CCCC STUDIES IN WRITING & RHETORIC

Edited by Victor Villanueva, Washington State University

The aim of the CCCC Studies in Writing & Rhetoric (SWR) Series is to influence how we think about language in action and especially how writing gets taught at the college level. The methods of studies vary from the critical to historical to linguistic to ethnographic, and their authors draw on work in various fields that inform composition—including rhetoric, communication, education, discourse analysis, psychology, cultural studies, and literature. Their focuses are similarly diverse—ranging from individual writers and teachers, to work on classrooms and communities and curricula, to analyses of the social, political, and material contexts of writing and its teaching.

SWR was one of the first scholarly book series to focus on the teaching of writing. It was established in 1980 by the Conference on College Composition and Communication (CCCC) in order to promote research in the emerging field of writing studies. As our field has grown, the research sponsored by SWR has continued to articulate the commitment of CCCC to supporting the work of writing teachers as reflective practitioners and intellectuals.

We are eager to identify influential work in writing and rhetoric as it emerges. We thus ask authors to send us project proposals that clearly situate their work in the field and show how they aim to redirect our ongoing conversations about writing and its teaching. Proposals should include an overview of the project, a brief annotated table of contents, and a sample chapter. They should not exceed 10,000 words.

To submit a proposal, please register as an author at www.editorial manager.com/nctebp. Once registered, follow the steps to submit a proposal (be sure to choose SWR Book Proposal from the drop-down list of article submission types).

COLLABORATIVE LEARNING AS DEMOCRATIC PRACTICE

A HISTORY

Mara Holt
Ohio University

Conference on College
Composition and
Communication

NCTE

National Council of
Teachers of English

Staff Editor: Bonny Graham
Manuscript Editor: Lee Erwin
Series Editor: Victor Villanueva
Interior Design: Mary Rohrer
Cover Design: Mary Rohrer and Lynn Weckhorst

NCTE Stock Number: 07300; eStock Number: 07317
ISBN 978-0-8141-0730-0; eISBN 978-0-8141-0731-7

It is the policy of NCTE in its journals and other publications to provide a forum for the open discussion of ideas concerning the content and the teaching of English and the language arts. Publicity accorded to any particular point of view does not imply endorsement by the Executive Committee, the Board of Directors, or the membership at large, except in announcements of policy, where such endorsement is clearly specified.

NCTE provides equal employment opportunity (EEO) to all staff members and applicants for employment without regard to race, color, religion, sex, national origin, age, physical, mental or perceived handicap/disability, sexual orientation including gender identity or expression, ancestry, genetic information, marital status, military status, unfavorable discharge from military service, pregnancy, citizenship status, personal appearance, matriculation or political affiliation, or any other protected status under applicable federal, state, and local laws.

Every effort has been made to provide current URLs and email addresses, but because of the rapidly changing nature of the Web, some sites and addresses may no longer be accessible.

Library of Congress Cataloging-in-Publication Data

Names: Holt, Mara, 1951– author.
Title: Collaborative learning as democratic practice : a history / Mara Holt.
Description: Urbana, Illinois : National Council of Teachers of English, 2017. | Series: CCCC Studies in writing & rhetoric | Includes bibliographical references and index.
Identifiers: LCCN 2017023515 (print) | LCCN 2017045987 (ebook) | ISBN 9780814107317 | ISBN 9780814107300(pbk.) | ISBN 9780814107317 (ebook)
Subjects: LCSH: Group work in education—United States—History. | Group work in education—Social aspects. | Progressive education—United States—History. | Democracy and education—United States—History.
Classification: LCC LB1032 (ebook) | LCC LB1032 .H663 2017 (print) | DDC 371.3/6—dc23
LC record available at https://lccn.loc.gov/2017023515

To Ken Bruffee and Jim Berlin

CONTENTS

MY FIRST FORMAL INTERACTION WITH COLLABORATIVE learning was at Kenneth Bruffee's Brooklyn College Institute in Peer Tutor Training and Collaborative Learning in 1980. I was a writing lab director at Alabama State University, and Bruffee's FIPSE-funded project was for the purpose of disseminating his tutor-training program nationally. Bruffee had "discovered" collaborative learning while training peer tutors as a writing program director at Brooklyn College in the wake of open admissions in the CUNY system. To understand the intellectual growth tutors experienced in his course, he had taken philosophy classes and learned about the seeds of what we would come to know as social constructivism. The Brooklyn College Institute was in some sense a Deweyan think tank: theory and practice in constant reciprocal interaction. As institute fellows, we acted both as students of Bruffee's training class and as teachers discussing our experiences, eventually engaging in reading groups focused on Lev Vygotsky, Clifford Geertz, Richard Rorty, Thomas Kuhn, John Dewey, and Paulo Freire. I met Peter Elbow, who participated as official evaluator for the institute. There were two more summer workshops and a conference at Yale, at which Stanley Fish was a keynote speaker. Along with Bruffee, I continued to collaborate with institute fellows Carol Stanger, John Trimbur, Harvey Kail, and Peter Hawkes. We published together, organized conferences at Bard College, and met often at CCCC. In 2008 Harvey Kail edited a special issue of the *Writing Center Journal* in honor of Bruffee's work. Most of us contributed to that issue, based on our experience in the institute. Kail's ("Innovation and Repetition") and Hawkes's ("Vietnam Protests") articles in that issue are significant historical readings of the institute and its material and political origins.

These experiences motivated me to pursue a PhD at the University of Texas at Austin, where I was fortunate to work with Greg

Myers in the year before he left for England. We argued about consensus and the relationship between theory and practice, and I learned from him. My fellow graduate students Hugh Burns, Valerie Balester, Kay Halasek, Fred Kemp, Wayne Butler, and Joyce Locke Carter developed Daedalus software, which created the first (preweb) networked computer classroom based on collaborative principles. While I interacted productively, if briefly, with Greg Myers and my Daedalus peers, the most significant influence on my historical work was James Berlin, who was visiting professor from the University of Cincinnati for a year. We used the prepublication manuscript of his book *Rhetoric and Reality* (SWR, 1987) as the textbook in the class I took with him. I talked him into adding Bruffee to his list of social-epistemic rhetors in the last chapter. Berlin shared my interest in the relationship between theory and pedagogy, and he taught me about ideology. His book showed me the excitement and significance of history. Lester Faigley, whose work was also influenced by his relationship with Berlin during that year, was my dissertation director, and Berlin, who left after one year for Purdue, served as a member of my committee.

When I began the historical work for my own manuscript, I was surprised to find that collaborative pedagogy had not been only an innovation of Bruffee's, but it had been also welcomed as an innovation in the 1920s, the 1950s, the 1970s, the 1990s (in networked computer scholarship), and most recently in current research on wikis. I found that with each mini-renaissance, collaborative pedagogies have been hailed as a democratic breakthrough. Working with then–graduate student Matthew Vetter, I saw that wiki scholars who cited Bruffee and Trimbur were not aware of the arc of hope and disappointment represented in the networked computer scholarship—for instance, Faigley (*Fragments* 1992), Romano (1993), and Regan (1993). I decided that this book could make a contribution.

ACKNOWLEDGMENTS

I THANK THOSE WHO HAD AN ENORMOUS IMPACT ON MY WORK: Kenneth Bruffee, Peter Elbow, James Berlin, Lester Faigley, Leon Anderson, and Victor Villanueva.

I am particularly grateful to the SWR reviewers of this project, Krista Ratcliffe and Deborah Holdstein, for their excellent and timely questions, and for Victor Villanueva, for shepherding me through this process and more. I am privileged to have had the expertise of NCTE editor Bonny Graham, as well as that of a freelance copy editor, during the final phase of this project.

Former fellows of the Brooklyn College Institute in Peer Tutor Training and Collaborative Learning who have enriched my work and my life include Harvey Kail, John Trimbur, Peter Hawkes, Carol Stanger, Ron Maxwell, and Marcia Silver. Many thanks to Harvey Kail for his valuable advice on writing center scholarship.

Thanks to Ohio University for supporting me with a Faculty Fellowship Leave. Matthew Vetter was indispensable to me as an expert on wiki scholarship. Gratitude to Paul Jones, Ayesha Hardison, Amanda Hayes, and especially Beth Daniell for encouragement. Thanks to Allison Ricket for keeping my priorities straight and to Linda Scott for showing me how.

Special thanks to Claudia Auger, research assistant and editor extraordinaire, who stuck with me through several revisions with cheerfulness and excellence beyond measure. And gratitude to Devan Murphy, who graciously worked with me in the final stages.

My mother, Marguerite Holt, inspired me with her intelligence, love, and unremitting faith. My brother, Jack Holt, helped me structure a summer's work by reading and responding to my work. My colleague Albert Rouzie contributed words and labor and time.

Loving appreciation to my partner, Albert, and dogs Lizzy and Sadie (and before them, Chewy) for succor and the pleasures of ordinary life.

1

Introduction and Overview

> [P]ractice is never natural or neutral; there is always a theory in
> place, so that the first job of any teacher of criticism is to bring
> the assumptions that are in place out in the open for scrutiny.
>
> —Robert Scholes, *Textual Power* (1985)

COLLABORATIVE LEARNING CAN BE DEFINED LOOSELY AS A pedagogy
that organizes students to work together in groups. It takes a variety
of forms. It may, for instance, entail students working together on a
project, copyediting one another's writing, solving a specific intellectual task together, participating in electronic class discussions,
or as a group providing encouragement for individual writers. All
cases of collaborative pedagogy include some form of interaction
among students. I do not wish to define the concept more narrowly
than this, since my purpose here is to explore variation in the practice and theory of collaborative pedagogy.[1]

A shift toward student-centered approaches has infused standard
assumptions about teaching writing, so that collaborative learning
has diffused into mainstream curricula, along with process pedagogy, to produce a conventional pedagogical protocol: freewrite,
draft, peer review, revise, hand in. Students are routinely taught
how to read others' writing. Teachers handle class discussion in
ways that create more engagement among students. Collaboration
is a standard part of computer pedagogy. And wikis, or collaborative texts modeled after Wikipedia, are becoming a popular classroom assignment.[2]

Proponents of collaborative learning claim that students learn
critical judgment and problem-solving skills and are socialized
into an academic discipline (Bruffee). They learn to resist (Kail

and Trimbur). They become empowered, learn conflict-resolution skills, and open their minds (Schniedewind). Proponents of computer-mediated collaboration claim that students learn the process of how communities form beliefs and change authority structures (Zappen, Gurak, and Doheny-Farina) by further decentralizing the role of teacher and centralizing peer interaction (Harasim). Collaborative pedagogy can help to overcome racism by giving voice to diverse participants and managing conflicts (Hertz-Lazarowitz), which increases students' literacy of difference (Blair). It creates opportunities for students to communicate, mentor one another, and become good citizens (Zuckerman).

Although there is a great deal of overlap, different versions of collaborative practice have different goals. We may practice collaboration under the assumption that we are inviting our students to participate in the creation of knowledge. Or we may believe that we are doing something very different, such as providing the conditions through which individual creativity can be released or raising our students' awareness about oppressive social structures. We may be trying to raise their self-esteem, provoke reflection, or train them to be future workers. Or we may not really think about what we're teaching our students through our pedagogy. If we are unconscious about our practices, we may be giving our students mixed messages, such as a teacher who wants to give students authority but micromanages them in groups.

Specific goals have varied historically, as well as across individual classrooms. Although collaborative learning is often practiced as standard boilerplate writing pedagogy, it has a distinctive twentieth-century history associated with American pragmatist philosophy. In the scholarship I found describing 1930s collaborative practices, for example, students were taught to cooperate with one another for social and economic survival in a time of no jobs. Group work in the late 1950s took some responsibility off the teachers for the increased student population of baby boomers. In the 1960s, collaborative learning and peer tutoring helped beleaguered teachers cope with open admissions. This led in the 1970s to collaboration in support of students unpacking the writing process, on the one hand, and protesting the Vietnam War, on the other. In the 1980s and 1990s, collaborative practice represented socially constructed knowledge in a time of postmodern epistemological uncertainty, a method to question the dominant ideologies of class and gender, and new notions of textuality exposed by electronic media. In the twenty-first century we are venturing into collaborations that recognize the contributions of objects and companion species.

A historical scan reveals a rich diversity of practices and can give us the distance necessary to examine our own practices. I take a historical approach to the study of collaborative learning for three reasons. Collaborative learning takes place in a particular context that must be understood and worked from for the practice to make any sense. Furthermore, collaborative learning has been underhistoricized, with the result that achievements have not built upon one another, but rather have emerged intermittently in the literature with the self-consciousness of repetitive spontaneous innovations. Finally, pragmatist philosophy, which offers the best rationale for collaborative pedagogy and has a long and productive relationship with it, depends upon dialectical connections among practice, theory, and material circumstances, to which a historical approach is crucial.

Teachers and historians in composition studies can benefit from knowing this history because our own practices are also historically situated. I argue that the effectiveness of collaborative learning is related to teachers' goals in using it, and that its practice is not separable from its historical and ideological situation. I use an analytical framework of knowledge, power, and social relations to understand various practices in their historical situations. I believe that a lack of awareness of the ideologies that saturate teachers' practices can subvert teachers' intentions and support a dysfunctional or antidemocratic environment for student learning. A book that documents the historical uses of collaborative practices can enable teachers to build on its earlier constructions, to analyze pedagogical moves in historical circumstances of cultural and political shifts, and to be more deliberate about what we do in our classrooms.

SITUATED MATERIAL CONTEXTS
FOR COLLABORATIVE LEARNING

A brief look at scholarship in relationship to context reveals some situational diversity in collaborative practices. For instance, Kenneth Bruffee's descriptions of collaborative practice are based in Brooklyn College, where his assumption is that differences among students don't need to be coaxed into expression, but rather constructively engaged. Lester Faigley faced a less pleasant version of this, describing one of his early computer-mediated classrooms as outrageously out of hand in his book *Fragments of Rationality* and showing concern about his students' racist, sexist discourse. Marilyn Cooper, in "Postmodern Possibilities in Electronic Conversations," sees Faigley's students' conflict as productive, even refreshing, perhaps because she was teaching a relatively homogeneous group of science majors in the Upper Peninsula of Michigan, a place where differences among students' beliefs may be more nuanced. Nevertheless, the focus on difference or consensus that has been debated in conversations in the discipline is often surprisingly devoid of attention to the material conditions and even the specific practices of the pedagogy at hand.

The material conditions of technology have had a significant impact on collaborative practices. Indeed, both Cooper's and Faigley's practices can be read as responses to the sudden new freedom students appropriated when their collaborative interactions were freed from spoken interaction, the classroom site at which teacher authority was ingrained in them from a hundred-year history of teacher control. The quick dance of keyboard response drives discourse more immediately than the spoken word. Its relative anonymity and simultaneity, in my experience, sometimes morphs a shy, obedient student into an outlaw subject. For a while, nonetheless, the readers and writers of the journal *Computers and Writing*—much like early face-to-face collaboration enthusiasts—saw in electronic collaboration a free space for egalitarian interaction. This is the context in which Faigley voiced his initial surprise and concern.

My fascination with physical, material contexts for pedagogical discussions and hands-on practices started in 1980 in the contrast between the Brooklyn College Summer Institute and my home institution, Alabama State. The institute fellows sat in a classroom high up in the CUNY Graduate School on 42nd Street (the pre-Giuliani pornographic version) doing collaborative tasks in the mornings and relating them to group dynamics and philosophy in the afternoons. My home context was a vibrant but overwhelmed HBCU that had sent me to New York soon after requiring tutoring for all of its twelve hundred first-year students in a writing lab that I had been hired to create without any funding for tutors. Both situations had their origin in the Civil Rights Movement, but the needs, the culture, and the material conditions were in striking contrast.

COLLABORATIVE LEARNING AS A SERIES OF PARALLEL INNOVATIONS

In addition to my interest in situated history, my second reason for pursuing a historical approach to this book is that many forms of collaborative practice don't talk to one another, and indeed don't necessarily know one another exist, and this happens synchronically as well as diachronically. Part of this is the nature of academic publishing in the discipline. In English studies, and thus in composition, practices and theories don't necessarily build on what came before, but may react against it and look toward innovation. This is particularly true for collaborative learning, which has been intermittently lost and found, rather than built upon, over the course of the twentieth century. There is much scholarship on collaborative practices in the 1920s and 1930s, for instance, but very little in the 1940s and 1950s. When collaborative learning is mentioned in the 1950s, it is without reference to or knowledge of the earlier practices, but rather as an epiphany. Collaborative pedagogies emerge in the scholarship again in the late 1960s and 1970s and come to flower in the 1980s. But in the 1990s, when teachers begin struggling with the pedagogical implications of computer classrooms, they treat issues of student collaboration and teacher authority as if they're brand-new problems, and they renew the cyclical process of reinventing the wheel. This has also happened in wiki scholarship.

COLLABORATIVE LEARNING
AND PHILOSOPHICAL PRAGMATISM

The third reason for a historical approach is that collaborative learning is historically aligned with American pragmatism, which guided John Dewey's influence on education throughout the twentieth century. Pragmatism remains the best guide to collaborative practice because of Dewey's extensive and unsurpassed work on the relationship between practice and theory in educational settings. It grounds, rather than limits, collaborative practice, and it offers a way to talk about all its varieties and their different situations. Issues that chronically concern teachers can be productively viewed in the context of the following four pragmatist principles. The first is that theory and practice must be connected, that they entail and reinforce each other. The second is that knowledge is fundamentally social and that collaborative interpretation is authoritative. One important premise of this second principle is that the self is a social product, or perhaps more accurately process. The third principle is that the most important, indeed crucial, component of education is growth in critical thinking. Closely related to the third principle is the fourth, that democracy and education require active social participation. In *Democracy and Education,* Dewey argues for education as a way to democratically reconstruct society, to prepare citizens for participation (20–22).

Pragmatist principles provide several suggestive leads regarding the most important avenues of investigation on this topic. These foci of attention include (1) power/authority issues, (2) social relations, and (3) conceptions of knowledge. These show up in teachers' definitions of knowledge and who has access to it; authority in the classroom and who has it; definitions of the self or subject; design of tasks, including structuring relationships among students; the nature of the relationship between individual freedom and social responsibility; the theme of democracy; the link between collaborative learning and social/political currents; the context of collaborative learning in the institution in which it is practiced; and the effectiveness of collaborative learning in meeting academic goals. Regardless of the variety of situations and practices, however, there are a few conditions generally in place when collaborative learning is successful. These include well-designed tasks, the freedom for students to complete the work collectively, and a method for holding students accountable.

Chapter 2 addresses collaborative practices that began in the early twentieth century progressive movement in education spurred by John Dewey's project to reform society by revising educational practice. Depression-era 1930s collaborative practices most closely approximated Dewey's intentions to provide education for participatory democracy. And then with the rise of general education, World War II, and the advent of the Cold War, the few collaborative pedagogies in the literature were based either on the group-dynamics research at the intersection of psychology and education or on the labor-saving, antiprogressive pedagogies that anticipated the effect of the baby boom on college enrollments. Although the 1930s show the most successful collaborative pedagogies in the early twentieth century, a comparison with the 1950s shows the significant difference between collaborative learning as inspired by Dewey and collaborative learning as a rejection of Dewey.

In Chapter 3 I argue that although Dewey and collaborative methods had lost popularity in a previous era of conformity, they blossomed again because of the protest movements that helped jumpstart the area of rhetoric and composition. A consequence of civil rights protest was the sudden implementation of open admissions in New York in 1970, which led to peer tutoring as one of many creative ideas to foster democracy systemically and in the classroom. As people realized the importance of democratic practices of citizenship, students gained some control over their education, and teachers developed methods to structure student participation. Using a historical and ideological framework, I examine the prominent methods such as peer tutoring, antiestablishment pedagogy (including the Happening), and the rise of writing-support groups.

Chapter 4 I devote to Peter Elbow, Kenneth Bruffee, Ira Shor, and antiracist pedagogy. Although student group work would likely have continued into the late twentieth century in some form, Elbow and Bruffee—both influenced by Dewey—are largely responsible for the way we think about and practice collaborative learning today. Their groundbreaking work came directly out of the material conditions of the 1960s. Their work not only made a large impact on the development of the field, but that influence continues. Without them, collaborative pedagogy might not have been as powerful a component of everyday writing instruction as it is today. Shor's pedagogy fulfilled Dewey's radical principles, because it grew from his focus on working-class pedagogy, which is designed to make students aware of economic injustice. I conclude Chapter 4 with a brief section on race and racism, partly to point out what's missing from the mainstream collaborative work.

Chapter 5 begins with the Marxian feminist work of Nancy Schniedewind and Carolyn Shrewsbury in the 1980s and moves to twenty-first-century feminist pedagogies that shift the collective power from "community" to "alliance." Schniedewind and Shrewsbury embody Dewey's project of influencing participatory democracy through education with detailed attention to practice designed to prepare students to bring feminist action to their political lives and workplaces when they graduate. Amie Macdonald and Susan Sánchez-Casals's *Twenty-First-Century Feminist Classrooms: Pedagogies of Identity and Difference* grapples with democracy-promoting practices in an environment of incommensurable differences, revealing the influence of pragmatist philosophy working in an environment of the shifting diversity of student populations and transnational concerns. The collaborative practices described in Chapter 5, along with the work of Shor and scholars on race, attempt to empower students collectively to become aware of, and potentially to do something about, inequities in class, race, and gender. I argue that the feminist collaborative pedagogies of Schniedewind and *Twenty-First-Century Feminist Classrooms* offer an extension of Dewey's vision and a response to the changing demographics and political needs of the twenty-first century.

Bruffee's work started in the writing center and continues in the alliances formed with European writing programs in the International Writing Center Association. His writing center in Brooklyn fostered his influential version of collaborative learning, and his Brooklyn College Summer Institute served as a seedbed for writing center directors nationally. One of those directors, Harvey Kail, has been influential in his work with teachers in emerging post-Wall democracies. The International Writing Centers Association is at the forefront of transnational work on pedagogy in the field of rhetoric and composition. At the same time, technological change is revolutionizing the way we write as well as what counts as writing. Writing centers are struggling with redefining their practices with new technological challenges and possibilities.

Participatory democracy has been part of the discourse of computer-mediated instruction from the introduction of computers into the classroom in the late twentieth century to the current blossoming of the wiki. In Chapter 7, I argue that Bruffee's collaborative learning theory was an integral part of the early networked classrooms at the University of Texas, which influenced the development of electronic collaboration. Lester Faigley and the group of graduate students who were trained in that program published prolifically, producing significant advances in the field as a result of those experiences. Additionally, pragmatist collaborative theory forms much of the early wiki scholarship. Both strands—networked classrooms and the wiki—have a pragmatist lineage and a familiarity with the cracks in network egalitarianism.

A NOTE ON METHOD

My documentation and analysis of collaborative pedagogy in Chapters 2 and 3 is based primarily on an examination of articles in three major English journals that historically have devoted substantial space to the topic of composition. The journals and years examined are *English Journal* (1912–38), *College English* (1939–86), and *College Composition and Communication* (1950–86).[3] In Chapters 4 and 5 I expanded my source list as the field has expanded and scattered to some extent. I have made use of search databases and delved into other journals such as *Computers and Composition, Radical Teacher, Rhetoric Review, Women's Studies Quarterly,* and various education journals.

I have read these texts on two levels. First, I have read them as information about what was being published, what the discourse of the community was in terms of progressive pedagogy. Second, I have read these texts hermeneutically through the lenses of various social theories, theories of identities, epistemologies, and ideologies. Finally, I have privileged those discourses that are drawn upon in the field of composition studies, and I have chosen to focus on the dominant threads in the field at a particular moment, rather than the minority voices. Suffice it to say that progressive pedagogy is, more often than not, a minority voice itself.

2

Collaborative Pedagogy in the Era of Progressive Education

WHILE CHAPTER 1 ESTABLISHED THE DEFINITIONS, METHOD, and scholarly contexts for this study, this chapter addresses collaborative practices in the first half of the twentieth century that bear some relationship to the progressive education movement spurred by John Dewey's work in reformist education and politics. Depression-era 1930s collaborative practices most closely approximated Dewey's intentions to provide education for participatory democracy. And then with the rise of general education, World War II, and the advent of the Cold War, the waning collaborative pedagogies were based either on the group-dynamics research at the intersection of psychology and education or on the labor-saving, antiprogressive pedagogies that anticipated the effect of the baby boom on college enrollments. The contrast between the 1930s and 1950s pedagogy shows the significant difference between collaborative learning in support of Dewey's goals and that in resistance to them. In this chapter I argue that Dewey's American pragmatism is a measuring rod by which we can evaluate collaborative pedagogy in support of democracy—both historically and theoretically. Attention to Dewey is important because his vision of education as a force for democracy continues to influence educators. In this chapter, then, I first demonstrate how Dewey's guiding principles for education offer a rationale for collaborative learning; I then follow the rise

A portion of this chapter was previously published in "Knowledge, Social Relations, and Authority in Collaborative Practices of the 1930s and the 1950s," *College Composition and Communication* 44.4 (1993): 538–55. Used with permission.

and fall of the progressive education movement by examining collaborative practices in the 1930s and in the 1950s.

JOHN DEWEY

Although Dewey never used the term *collaborative,* as far as I know, the best principles of collaborative learning are reflected in his commitment to carefully designed work that fostered active student participation toward a democratic goal. The contribution of Dewey's pragmatist thought to a discussion of collaborative learning assumes a dialectical relationship between theory and practice, a social epistemology and subjectivity, and democratic authority. David Russell has cogently paraphrased Dewey's social epistemology in the following words: "Each of us has a unique sociocultural heritage: a history of interactions with others and events which produces individual, *original* adaptations and transformations of one's self and others and events" (178). Dewey was fascinated with the emerging scientific method, with its assumption that experience can be tested, and that the consequences of that testing determine the next step in the experiment. For Dewey's project of wide-scale educational reform, having students act and then experience the consequences of their actions enables learning to take place that is tested by experience.

Dewey drew from his notion of experience two criteria—interaction and continuity. As an alternative to absolute truth and banked knowledge, interaction and continuity evoke movement, a process, fluid and recursive, not stable—significant characteristics of a vital conception of experience, one that for Dewey could embrace the change that he experienced and foresaw in the culture around him. It was important for Dewey that students have a grasp of the way society functions not only to make school more engaging, but also to prepare them to be responsible citizens in the democracy he wanted to use education to promote.

Extrapolating from Marx, Dewey saw students as alienated workers when they were disconnected from the consequences of their work (*Human Nature* 270–71). If students could understand learning as their own participation in the social drama, they could begin to see the point in what they were supposed to know (*Democracy and Education* 135). Dewey urged teachers to quit talking at students and instead to create conditions in which students could work through problems cumulatively and progressively and see the results of their achievement ("Individuality and Experience" 1). His Laboratory School at the University of Chicago was an attempt to set up conditions for teachers so they could do just that.

Relevant to my study of collaborative learning, then, are some of Dewey's key principles:

- Independent, critical thinking necessitates focused and reflective thinking, or "the power to hold problems, questions, before the mind" (*School and Society* 149).
- The student's task should not be fabricated, but real. Otherwise, the excitement of accomplishing something is gone (*School and Society* 119).
- Imitation should be used very carefully, not as a model for potential behavior, but only as a way to guide behavior already initiated by the student (*School and Society* 124).

Not all of these principles appear in collaborative practices of the first half of the twentieth century, but they are important reminders of the goals of collaborative learning, lest the group work we practice become as stale as the banking model that Dewey, and later Paulo Freire, opposed.

Dewey promoted education as a tool for reforming society, though he recognized that radical educational reform required a concomitant change in the US economic and social structure. He wanted to harness the potential of education to provide citizens the skills, knowledge, and habits they needed to govern themselves, both for their own autonomy and for the revitalization of society. Students and workers should be taught how to work together creatively by participating democratically in their schools and workplaces, because, Dewey maintained, authoritarian methods will impede the growth of individuals and society.

Such education, Dewey argued, required the intelligent leadership of the teacher.[4] The teacher's task is to create conditions in which students can work through problems cumulatively and see the results of their achievement (*Experience and Education* 77–78), thus ensuring not only interaction, but also continuity. Dewey cautioned, however, that teachers cannot give students absolute freedom; students must be taught how to structure learning (64–65). Dewey's teacher has a difficult job: to set up constraints that encourage intelligent freedom.

As Robert Westbrook has noted, Dewey was critical of the prevailing "negative liberal" depiction of freedom as a simple lack of constraint, arguing that a more meaningful conception of freedom recognized not only "freedom from" but also "freedom to"—that is, freedom to positively enable self-realizing activities, made possible through the personal development of knowledge, skills, and habits acquired from association with others (42–51). It made as little sense to set students free to explore their own ideas spontaneously as it did to educate them through the exclusive use of "fact-centered" recitation and lecture. Each extreme, as Dewey explained in *Experience and Education,* was a misunderstanding of the dynamic interplay between individual impulse and historical situation necessary to both intellectual and societal growth. That Dewey has so often been misrepresented as fostering "student-centered" education, as Russell points out, is partly a result of the unfortunate tendency to identify him with almost everything "progressive" (174).

It is important to note what Dewey was reacting to. Nineteenth-century education had been designed to train an educated, middle-class meritocracy. Educational success was determined though mass testing, and the goal was to train workers for corporate employers. Writing instruction was not about making good arguments, but rather about mastering conventions of usage and style. Dewey harked back to the classical goals of educating students for the public good.

Predictably, collaborative practices based loosely on Dewey's progressive ideas took on some of the prevailing ideological assumptions of the particular historical era. In the environment of the

1920s' exuberance of riches and of the emerging scientific method of experimentation, educators wrote about student group work using business and engineering metaphors and analogies. Their practices focused on either the individual student (with the group as a resource) or a group project with no structured role for the individual (for example the Dalton Plan and the Project Method).[5] The 1930s' crash of the stock market and subsequent Great Depression brought about collaborative practices described as necessary to the survival of the country. In an atmosphere of the Cold War and anti-collective fear-mongering, collaborative pedagogy in the 1940s and 1950s was employed to detect propaganda and, reluctantly, to accommodate the enrollment "floods" of postwar and baby-boomer students. Later, amid Vietnam War protests and the Civil Rights Movement of the 1960s and 1970s, collaborative learning returned to its Deweyan roots, as the discipline of rhetoric and composition established itself as an area in English studies with a particular interest in pedagogy.

COLLECTIVE ACTION AND THE DEPRESSION ERA

This is like life, and the students know it.
—Frank Earl Ward, "Social Ideals in
Freshman English" (1930)

For the teacher of the 1920s, life was—ideally—a successful business relationship. The economy was flourishing in the 1920s, and business was a friend of education. But the 1930s Depression changed the relationship of business to education. Many Americans saw business as having failed them. In discussions of collaborative pedagogy, the business metaphor vanished, replaced by "co-operation." Collaborative pedagogy continued to be represented as "lifelike," but life had changed. Social engineering had not worked. There was a lack of trust in authority. As envisioned by college English teachers who wrote on collaborative practice, "life" in the 1930s was a grassroots cooperative enterprise.

Much collaborative practice in the 1930s espoused a collective, democratic spirit consonant with some Depression-era politics and the prevalence of leftist sympathies among academics. The 1930s' rationales for collaborative learning were in line with social-reconstructionist sympathies among intellectuals such as Dewey, George S. Counts, and Harold Rugg (who published a bestselling series of leftist social studies texts).[6] The literary counterparts to Dewey, Counts, and Rugg were socialist authors such as John Dos Passos and literary critics such as Marxist Granville Hicks, populist Vernon Louis Parrington, and eclectic pragmatist Kenneth Burke. Although leftists did not constitute a majority in English departments in the 1930s, they competed with humanist scholars and early New Critics to define the discipline. And the impact of progressive education on writing instruction was felt not only in collaborative classroom practices but also in the administration of first-year English programs (Berlin, *Rhetoric and Reality* 64).[7]

In the United States there was broad cultural support for social reform beyond the academy, and successful collective action in this period made socialism more than an intellectual pipe dream. First, there were strikes for union representation. In 1934 there were 1,856 strikes (Manchester 161); in 1937, 4,720—82 percent of which ended in favor of unions (195). Second, there were farmers' foreclosure riots, which involved embargoes and violence against bankruptcy lawyers and judges (70). Finally, in anticipation of U.S. involvement in World War II, there were student antiwar demonstrations. In 1935, 150,000 students participated in a national Student Strike for Peace. Pacifist students were members of the Student League for Industrial Democracy (SLID), a forerunner of Students for a Democratic Society (SDS), the popular antiwar organization in the Vietnam era (152). In short, many students and educators in the Depression-era 1930s supported radical democratic reform, and it is clear now that teachers who used collaborative practices in the 1930s were in some sense responding to widespread cultural assumptions. Returning to my framework of knowledge, power/authority, and social relations, all of it reflected some version of social interaction. In many cases teachers facilitated students' construction of knowledge, the authority of powerful individuals was not valorized, and social relations among students were horizontal and friendly. *Communism* was a friendly word.

Specifically, teachers consistently defined knowledge as interactional or relational. Moving far from the 1920s' focus on IQ tests, for instance, in 1932 R. L. Lyman at the University of Chicago defined intelligence as "the ability to see relationships" (94); four years later Stanford professor Holland Roberts modified this definition to "the capacity to see social relationships" (200). Charles Rossier of Culver Military Academy, discussing the effects of peer-editing groups in his composition classroom, emphasized the value of the social skills acquired by his students, mentioning subject matter almost as an aside. Frank Earl Ward, who taught a cross-disciplinary course in English and history at Macalester College in St. Paul, agreed with Rossier's focus on social skills, adding that group methods helped give his students knowledge of broad theoretical frameworks, rather than discrete, isolated facts ("Modern World Culture"). Students were often encouraged to participate in the negotiation of knowledge. At Florida State College for Women, G. L. Diffenbaugh used a group-outlining technique, whereby students presented their ideas to the class and then negotiated their value. Diffenbaugh wrote: "One of the most stimulating phases of communal outlining lies in the discussion evolving from the students' challenges and defenses of the ideas presented" (745). That Diffenbaugh articulates the rhetorical basis of group work is a move toward attention to students' relationships with one another that was missing in 1920s collaborative practices such as the Project Method.

That teachers in the 1930s took seriously the empowerment of their students is revealed in their careful structuring of classroom practices that enabled them to interact fruitfully with one another. These teachers encouraged students' interdependence while attempting to underplay their own authority. For example Elsie Carroll from Brigham Young, in a 1931 article titled "Freshening Freshman English," asked students "to forget that they were in a classroom, and to feel that they were with a group of friends in an informal gathering" (762). Initially the teacher took the role of facilitator of the discussion, but later she gave that role to one of the students. Instructors were consistently advised to leave the room or stay otherwise occupied while students were fulfilling their group tasks. In "Social Ideas in Freshman English" (1930), Ward taught his students to take on authority in three phases. First the instructor was to be the group leader, then he or she would appoint a student surrogate with the instructor in the room, and finally the students would meet together without the teacher. "If the instructor does not allow the class to lean upon him too heavily for suggestions," Ward said, "a genuine spirit of social responsibility gradually grows up" (303). In Diffenbaugh's collaborative outlining procedure, it was the class, not the teacher, who decided what went in and what stayed out. "Since communal outlining is valuable mainly for its training in . . . thinking, the instructor's attitude toward the discussion should be at this point of the procedure most liberal. I never intrude . . . except at the request of the students," Diffenbaugh explained (746). Diffenbaugh's rationale for abdicating the conventional role was intellectual growth for the students.

As with Kenneth Bruffee's 1980s collaborative learning, many teachers in the 1930s seemed to measure the success of their work by their students' gradually decreasing dependence on them, and conversely, their increasing dependence on each other, in line with what Karen Spear has referred to as "peer collaborat[ion]." Teachers encouraged their students in what Spear describes as "mutual generation and exploration of ideas," "equal status relationships," and "shared responsibility for achieving group task[s]" (58). Columbia University professor B. J. R. Stolper, for example, demonstrated support of students' interdependence in describing group work as successful when "the teacher returns to glance in through the door, [and] nobody pays him the least attention; [students] are unaware of him" (321). In line with Dewey's goals, then, many 1930s teachers consciously hoped that group work would give their students access to the rudiments of participatory democracy.

This conscious awareness of democratic goals is clear in several articles on pedagogy in the 1930s, which begin by offering a social approach to teaching English as part of a national economic remedy. In 1932, for instance, Lyman contended that "[t]he present economic disaster is partly the result of unrestricted individualism. . . . Everyone realizes that the progress of our civilization depends on real socialization. We must find ways of developing the group spirit of co-operation" (90). In 1933 a student of Rossier noted that the group process had taught him to be open to others' ideas (Rossier 29–30). Stolper in "The Group Poem" described a sense of communal responsibility for the product. The group poem, created by individuals, spawned individual poems (319). Individuality was nurtured by group process, according to Stolper.

This faith in the group's beneficent influence on the individual, however, was not unanimous. In the 1930s, much of the talk about the relationship of the individual to the group reflects a complicated coexistence, an anxious perception that one is always in danger of overwhelming the other. As if writers were afraid to upset a fragile equilibrium, they seemed to make certain not to end a sentence unless both words—*social* and *individual*—were in place. Ward's statement is an example: "We should select what we teach with the social ideal before us, and we should organize our classes about the individual—the individual thought of as part of a social group" ("Social" 299). In *English Journal* editor W. Wilbur Hatfield's 1933 survey of English teachers, the educational values that tied for second place were "citizenship activities" and the individual's "private, inner satisfactions" (538). (Social awareness through reading literature took first place.) Part of the "social ideal" in the 1930s college classroom was an acceptance of diversity. Edith Jones of Dayton Teachers College notes in "Teaching Conversation" (1931) that diversity in personality, social advantage, background, and "mental ability" is to be expected and, indeed, is invited in the collaborative classroom (217).

To some extent throughout the decade, but particularly toward the end, writers on collaborative practice voiced doubts about the success of balancing the roles of the group and the individual. Although students were consistently given free choice of topics and encouraged to follow their interests, Walter Barnes at New York University found it necessary to warn teachers that students' reactions to group experience would be varied, and that their private pursuits should be respected. Dora V. Smith at the University of Minnesota, who with Barnes had been an ardent supporter of collaboration, was concerned in 1937 that if a student were encouraged to take an interest in city or national issues, or to relate her experience too closely with the community, the student could lose a sense of personal meaning in her life (101). The attempts of some composition theorists in the 1930s to posit a pragmatist, socially based epistemology were in tension with their simultaneously held Romantic notions of the individual as a separate, autonomous being. What we find in 1930s practices is a blend of what we now think of as expressive and social rhetorics.[8]

Most 1930s pedagogy focused on individual and group processes equally, but made little use of Dewey's more thoroughly social framework for understanding the engagement between the two.[9] On Dewey's terms, as John Trimbur explains, "the social interaction of shared activity . . . [enables] individuals [to] realize their own power to take control of their situation by collaborating with others" ("Consensus" 604). Seeing the individual and the group as polar opposites, as many 1930s teachers did, ensures a constant anxiety about which formation is being privileged. This tension is further explained by a rift in the 1930s between radicals and moderates in the Progressive Education Association (PEA).[10] In 1932 George S. Counts gave a rousing speech to the PEA titled "Dare Progressive Education Be Progressive?" This speech, which echoed themes in a speech by Dewey to the PEA in 1928, both moved and divided the organization, influencing educators much as FDR's New Deal affected the US populace (Kliebard 196). It galvanized the PEA to try for more radical measures than just progressive pedagogy, such as improved working conditions for teachers, during a time when all teachers' salaries were cut as a result of the Depression, and some teachers worked for free in order to keep schools open. At the same time, Counts's speech, which espoused "indoctrination" of students toward socialist aims, divided radical and moderate factions, and, according to Lawrence Cremin, helped to lead ultimately to the demise of progressive education (258–70). The emphasis on students' personal goals that characterizes the literature toward the end of the 1930s may have been in some sense a reaction on the part of moderates to the radical faction of the PEA. Furthermore, with the

Hitler-Stalin pact in 1939, collective action began to be associated with totalitarianism in the United States.

Also a factor in the demise of a true progressive agenda was the rise of the general education movement, an effort to replace the progressive education movement with a series of basic courses that all college students would take in their first two years before proceeding to more specialized courses. These courses were general in two ways. One was that all students would take them. Two was that they were to teach essential truth, which is always the same "at any time, in any place, under any political, social, or economic conditions" (86), according to one of its champions, University of Chicago president Robert M. Hutchins. Hutchins and Dewey debated general education over the course of years in the journal *Social Frontier*.[11] While Dewey agreed with Hutchins about the fragmented state of education, he disagreed with Hutchins's transcendent notion of truth. Dewey's position is clear in the following excerpt from "President Hutchins' Proposals to Remake Higher Education":

> I would not intimate that the author has any sympathy with fascism. But basically his idea as to the proper course to be taken is akin to the distrust of freedom and the consequent appeal to some fixed authority that is now overrunning the world. There is implicit in every assertion of fixed and eternal first truths the necessity for some *human* authority to decide, in this world of conflicts, just what these truths are and how they shall be taught. This problem is conveniently ignored. . . . As far as I can see, President Hutchins has completely evaded the problem of who is to determine the definite truths that constitute the hierarchy. (103–4)

Dewey went on to propose an alternative solution to the crisis in education. Rather than seeking to escape contemporary problems by proposing the existence of eternal truths, Dewey argued that educational institutions should become more closely involved with the reconstruction of problematic social institutions. Dewey recognized the potential political problems involved in transforming educational institutions from their dependent, reactive position in society. "The immediate effect of such attention," he wrote, "would probably be withdrawal of donations of money" ("President" 104). Nonetheless, he contended, the only viable solution lay in connecting education to society rather than in withdrawing from society into a realm of eternal first principles based on classical literature. While Dewey and Hutchins were debating the University of Chicago's Great Books approach to general education, Harvard's James Bryant Conant was propagating a slightly different approach to general education, one based on nationalism. The first priority of general education, Conant maintained, should be the development of "a common set of values." He urged his readers to think "of the system of universal education as an instrument of national policy" (quoted in Graff 167).

THE COLD WAR ERA

> Our premise is not that group instruction is preferable to individual clinical procedure; rather, our contention is that, given a situation where there is no alternative, group instruction is not a hopeless way to solve the problem of college reading improvement.
>
> —U. B. Elliott and George Adrian Kuyper,
> "Remedial Reading—Group Treatment" (1940)

As James Berlin saw it, the democratic vision of the 1940s and 1950s was rhetorically based in individualism and a strong distrust of social influences (*Rhetoric and Reality* 109–10). If this is true, then the individual was not Dewey's creative thinker, but rather a stagnant repository of the values imposed by a higher authority and transmitted through education. This concept of education was at odds with Dewey's criteria of interaction and continuity. Democracy was redefined away from Dewey's sense of participation and toward a notion of expertise, an abstract democracy removed from the contributions of ordinary people. Dewey dropped out of the discourse during this period, and collaborative practice in the teaching of writing suffered a decline.[12]

Further, as I suggested earlier, the events surrounding the Second World War and the postwar panic about Communism in the United States had created a discourse of distrust concerning group action. As Donald Stewart has noted, the word *collaborator* had such repugnant associations that it was not possible to use it in a positive sense (66). By the late 1950s, leftist literary critics had lost the influence they had had in the 1930s. English studies, rather, maintained a peaceful coexistence between New Criticism and historical scholarship, which had become at best the "internal history" of the body of literature itself (Graff 188–89). The discipline's attempt "to detach itself from the social will and to ignore every other form of thought except as it can absorb it into its own technical apparatus" was representative of the late 1950s professional according to Harold Rosenberg (qtd. in Graff 199). The purpose of literature in a democracy was treated in a 1938 MLA document, "Statement of the Committee of Twenty-Four," which warns against privileging social values over individual ones: "The individual, thus submerged in the social mass, is merely a cipher, a helpless unit whose thought, feeling, and action are determined by impersonal forces over which he has little or no control. . . . Whatever the errors of rugged individualism in the economic sphere, the concept of political democracy assumes the efficacy of rugged individualism on the plane of the spirit" (qtd. in Berlin, *Rhetoric* 110). By the 1950s this representation of individualism was well established. In the wake of Nazism, Stalinism, World War II, and the consolidation of an objective view of knowledge, the group was no longer seen as a resource for the individual as it had been throughout most of the 1930s; it was now a veiled threat.[13]

Nevertheless, two versions of collaborative practice that surfaced in my research are worth comment for their philosophical antagonism to pragmatism and the implications that antagonism has for definitions of democracy, particularly around the issue of the authority of knowledge. One is the brief flowering of composition classes influenced by "group dynamics" in the early 1950s, drawn from the work of educational psychologists Kurt Lewin and Jerome Bruner. The other is an influential program called the Oregon Plan, which used student peer collaboration as a response to the post–World War II baby boom.

Group Dynamics

In some ways, group-dynamics pedagogy bears a resemblance to 1930s collaborative practice. Roles such as timekeeper and observer were assigned to students, and intragroup communication was attended to conscientiously. The group-dynamics proponents tried to promote democracy in classroom structure—even to the point of endeavoring to make the students' written work "one of the basic textbooks of the course" (Sorensen 162). Harold Briggs of the University of Southern California in his "Applications of the Principles of Group Dynamics in the College Classroom" described the value of his class in terms of chairs arranged in a circle, denoting the equality of everyone in the room (including the teacher). Briggs concluded that this structure reflects, "perhaps, that democracy is a good way of life and that we must learn how to make it work" (84–85). Elizabeth Kerr in 1952 described the final themes in her collaborative class as "gratifying" in the sense that "group interest and individual growth are manifest" (208). Quite in line with Lewin's work on group dynamics and with the democratic theme in these early fifties articles is a pamphlet published by the Educator's Washington Dispatch in Washington, DC. In "So You Appointed a Committee," one of "two lessons in group dynamics" found in the pamphlet, a bad leader is described as a policeman, a "results" man, or a laissez-faire leader. A good leader, on the other hand, knows group process and how to make it work.

A closer look at how group-dynamics proponents made it work reveals the postwar focus on expertise, or a hierarchical conception of democracy. The goal in that model was in some sense Fordist—for expert managers to figure out how democracy works best and then mass-produce it. For instance, group-dynamics pedagogy added the role of student "observer," whose job it was to evaluate the group process and make suggestions for improvement. The use of a single "observer," as opposed to general group analysis of process, is a departure from collaborative procedure in the 1930s (see

Jones's "Teaching Conversation"). To be fair, in the pamphlet describing group dynamics, the role of "group observer" is offered as a way to mitigate the authority of the leader and to make the group aware of its process (*Two Lessons* 5). However, it gave one student middle manager status, the power to represent the group to itself and to the teacher. The pedagogy that came out of group-dynamics theory also calls to mind a respect for scientific expertise. The point was that human interaction in groups could be engineered in accordance with immutable principles of human behavior, and the problem solver was the expert on scientific management, reminiscent of social engineering in the 1920s (see Holt's "Dewey"). Not surprisingly, group-dynamics research was strongly supported by the military and commercial enterprises, which found an affinity between their needs and this scientific paradigm.

The Demise of Progressive Education

By the late 1950s, progressive education had lost credibility for several reasons. In response to the war needs of the 1940s, an offshoot of progressive education called "life adjustment" had shifted attention toward a vocational and applied focus, ultimately deteriorating in the 1950s into an anti-intellectual parody of its former self—teaching such subjects as dating, relating to your parents, and picking a good dentist. Although not relevant to Dewey's educational goals, in the eyes of the public the life adjustment movement was linked to progressive education. A second factor that led to the unpopularity of progressive education was the rise of the military-industrial complex and its links to American education. The National Science Foundation and the National Defense Education Act were introduced as an incentive to science education and research in the service of advancing military technology. In this conservative postwar milieu, historian Arthur Bestor and others blamed progressive education for what they saw as a crisis in national education standards. The third important social force in the 1950s that weakened the position of progressive education was the unexpectedly increasing enrollments. Progressivism had been an expansionist movement in which social reconstructionists had called upon education to accomplish goals broader and more complex than the traditionally narrow academic mandate had required. And the 1950s brought an increase in technology, information, and complexity in world politics unparalleled in previous decades (Cremin 352). Meanwhile what Vincent Leitch calls the "massification of higher education" had dramatically increased college enrollments (150). Rather than expand the responsibilities of education, overwhelmed 1950s educators wanted to limit those responsibilities. The baby boom was the last straw.

The collaborative pedagogy that surfaced between 1940 and 1961 reflected one of two stances: the first, an attempt to wed pragmatist and positivist beliefs, was represented by the collaborative practice influenced by group dynamics; the second, more dominant stance, in active opposition to pragmatism, was characterized by an emphasis on teacher authority, on the individual's place in a hierarchy of knowledge, on clarity of thought and expression, and on a self-conscious appraisal of collaborative pedagogy as administratively functional, rather than educationally, philosophically, or politically reconstructive.

The Oregon Plan

The most influential collaborative practice of the 1950s, and definitely the most colorful, was Charlton Laird's "Oregon Plan," which was bandied about in *College English* and *College Composition and Communication* between 1956 and 1961. Laird, a linguist and former chair of the English Department at the University of Nevada, Reno, was for a short time a visiting professor at the University of Oregon. He worked with John Sherwood, Oregon's director of composition, to modify first-year English so that students would trade papers and write critiques of each other's papers, then respond to those critiques before revising the original papers and handing them in to the teacher (see Sherwood). This detailed and structured peer critique process anticipates Kenneth Bruffee's 1970s practice developed initially for training peer tutors. In fact, the initiating circumstances were similar. Bruffee's practice came out of the influx of students who entered New York's CUNY system in 1970 when admissions opened. And Laird's was a response to an anticipated staffing shortage caused by the advent of "baby boom" children into colleges in the 1960s. But the purposes of the two practices were different. For Bruffee, who embraced the work of Dewey and Paulo Freire in the wake of the 1960s Civil Rights and antiwar movements, the rationale for collaborative learning was intellectual growth. He had discovered that peer tutors trained in collaborative practices learned as much as their tutees. He strove to make students dependent on one another and thus capable of gaining authority through group interaction. Laird used the method apologetically, writing in a post-progressive Cold War era when Dewey had become a scapegoat and the practice of blackballing suspected Communists a reality. Laird's practice of collaborative learning subverted Dewey's goals of using education to promote activist democracy. It incentivized students' suspicion of one another in favor of dependence on an official authority figure. At the same time that Laird was writing the article (published in 1956) describing the plan, Senator Joseph McCarthy was holding hearings in Congress in which he pressured citizens to submit names of peers who might have been sympathetic to Communism.

In the Oregon Plan, teachers encouraged students to internalize the role of the teacher by exposing weaknesses in one another's writing. As a student said, "If the teacher marks something wrong on your paper, you think probably he knows, and you don't do much about it. But if a student marks your paper, you think maybe he's wrong and you can catch him at it, so you look it up" (Laird 134). In contrast to this practice, Dewey had implored teachers to design tasks to maximize students' autonomy and initiative in concert with others, warning that authoritarian methods restrain democratic impulses and ultimately inhibit the growth of society. By the early 1950s, however, Dewey's influence had waned, and the practices he had promoted had been distorted. In 1953, Bestor published *Educational Wastelands*, a critique of the "life adjustment movement" that had attached itself to progressive education.

Thus, pedagogically as well as politically, the ideological and epistemological environment that most 1950s teachers worked in conveyed the belief that group work was a pedagogical risk, and that they should maintain as much control as possible. Acknowledging that the weakest link in his system was the teacherless group sessions, Laird suggested that "the instructor may manage a sort of remote control by turning conference discussions to a review of the talk in the student group meeting" (135). Laird makes suggestions for times when "the instructor feels uncertain of his hold upon the class" and plans ways "to increase my control" by having students turn in reports of the student meetings (135). Laird's teacherless meeting was not teacherless for the sake of the students, as it had been in Ward's class in the 1930s (or, for that matter, in Peter Elbow's 1973 *Writing without Teachers*), but rather for the sake of the teacher. The teacher who had assiduously made herself scarce in 1930s collaborative practice was advised in a report on a workshop at the 1957 CCCC to provide continuous guidance and evaluation "by remaining throughout a full session in one group" ("Using Group Dynamics" 150). And the technique of group evaluation, which had been accomplished informally in the 1920s and 1930s by the groups themselves, and had given way in the early 1950s to the role of student "observer," became in the mid-1950s a tape recorder with the teacher present.

Laird's most prominent metaphor is *scrutiny*. "The students had learned," he wrote, "to scrutinize writing, other people's writing and eventually their own, as they had never scrutinized any writing before" (134). Students were in groups not primarily to challenge and defend ideas, but rather to speed up the process of correcting papers. There was much fear of inefficiency in this period, fear of "the blind leading the blind." Both Laird and Edwin Benjamin, who used the group method to teach literature classes, encouraged their students to make use of two allies—the textbook and the teacher.

Laird's and Benjamin's statements imply that peer groups will work if students can internalize the role of the teacher, the person with the clearest vision of knowledge. There is no discussion about the social conventions of writing, of knowledge as interactive, as we saw in the 1930s discourse. Authority is not an issue for discussion; it is taken for granted. This emphasis on expert authority is consistent with the purpose of collaborative learning for Laird and his colleagues: saving labor. Laird's article begins with a question:

> We started by asking ourselves what a section of freshman English costs in time. . . . We assumed that if I could teach the class in seven or eight hours without worse results than I should have expected from eleven hours, we could theoretically increase an instructor's load twenty-five to thirty percent without either him or his class suffering appreciably. (132)

Laird continued with his focus on saving time, noting that the method "permits an instructor to juggle his sections so that he can get whole days free, or mornings or afternoons free" (136). Laird went so far as to include a humorous chart in his article, noting the hours at which the instructor would be free to play golf. Laird's humor shows how much he wants to distance himself from anything that smacks of progressive education.

Laird proposed that "the procedure will permit a relatively small number of experienced faculty to direct the work of a very large number of inexperienced and inadequately prepared teachers to do better teaching than they would have done with the conventional system" (138). George Wykoff, in an article bluntly titled "Current Solutions for Teaching Maximum Numbers with Limited Faculty" (1958), referred to the "Student Participation Plan" as one way to make fewer teachers able to serve more students (78). Other time-savers mentioned were television, discussion sections, handbooks and exercise books, part-time staff graders, writing labs, and electronic theme readers. After the results of the experiment were tallied, Laird and Sherwood disagreed over whether the method saved time, but they agreed that the performance of the students and the general enthusiasm of both teachers and students rose much more than they had predicted. The major concern of the teachers in the 1920s, 1930s, and early 1950s (collaboration as an effective way to teach) was only a puzzling but pleasant side effect to

Laird and Sherwood. The advantages of the group method for the teacher, according to Edwin Benjamin, who tried the method with literature classes, were that it prepared the students for livelier class discussion, it allowed the teacher to more easily become "aware of student misconceptions," and it gave the teacher a break and was "to be recommended in moments of stress or strain, if he is suffering from a cold or (*et pudet et dicam*) a hangover" (123). As funny as this was when I first read it, I was fascinated imagining a cultural moment so saturated with anti-Communist rhetoric that this sort of thing could get published, that it was necessary to qualify one's regard for the pedagogy to that extent. It strengthened my commitment to an ideological awareness of pedagogical practices. I am curious about why the students were enthusiastic, what exactly they learned in "scrutinizing" peers' writing, and how those assumptions influenced them in other ways.

In addition to the denigrating humor, characteristic of the literature on collaborative pedagogy in the mid- to late 1950s is a concluding disclaimer. Laird's is representative, and somewhat surprising, given the enthusiasm he has unwittingly betrayed about collaborative pedagogy:

> None of us recommends this. We believe there is no substitute for a good teacher with plenty of time to do a thorough job. . . . But if the floods come, if the population watersheds continue to pour more and more untamed young upon us, we hope we have a method of stretching the levees a little, even though not enough. (138)

Probably the most telling response comes from the chair of the Department of English at the University of Oregon, where Sherwood was Director of Freshman English and Laird was visiting professor. Professor Souers, according to Laird, was pleased with the plan because he saw in it a way to gradually abolish first-year English.

Laird's ambivalence about collaborative practice can be understood in its historical situation. Indeed, even Laird's critics rebuked him not for being too harsh and authoritarian, but for being too soft and idealistic. George Herman, in his first response to Laird's

Oregon Plan, suspected that the plan wouldn't work because it would require too much devotion (and interest in composition) from the teacher. S. J. Sackett, in "Report on a Trial of the Oregon Plan," was furious at Laird because, in his estimation, the plan did not work. "There seems to me to be absolutely no saving in time," Sackett says: the groups were so noisy "that I had to go [in] and take charge"; students did a terrible job of "grading each other's papers"; and Sackett's objective testing showed that his "students don't learn much English by the Oregon plan" (45). Sackett concluded by accusing Laird of having become "infected with the educationist fallacy that teaching is a craft and involves a method that anyone can learn, if only you can find the right method" (45–46). Herman then took it upon himself to reply to Sackett, defending Laird against that description.

An article published in *College English* in 1961, the last year that the Oregon Plan is mentioned, sums up the era rather aptly. In "Freshman English in Sections of 150," Walker Gibson welcomes oversized composition classes as a pedagogical innovation. "This has not been a device for saving money (for it has saved none)," contends Gibson; "it has been a device for maintaining and improving standards by saving teaching talent" (501). Gibson's idea reflects the value attached to the expert. "The challenge," says Gibson, "probably appeals particularly to the sort of teacher who thinks of himself partly as an actor, and certainly the sight of such a vast captive audience is a heady experience for anyone." One disadvantage for the teacher, says Gibson, is that he doesn't get to know his students personally, since his teaching assistants hold all the office hours. On the other hand, notes Gibson, "he has also been spared some fairly impossible human relations" (502). Gibson's antiprogressive stance is reflected by his contrasting images of the teacher as an actor with a "vast captive audience" and the students as sometimes "impossible." Though many of us can at times identify with this sentiment, progressive educators are not likely to publish such descriptions without analysis. That Gibson does is a window into the environment for collaborative pedagogy in the 1950s.

Consistent with Laird's goal of "scrutinizing writing," Gibson sees the "scrutinizing" of teaching to be an advantage for the graduate teaching assistants: They are "subject to a kind of scrutiny and evaluation that no schedule of 'visitation' could approach, for they are almost constantly under the eye of their superior" (502). Coupled with the validation of "scrutiny" we see here an antiprogressive sense of knowledge and authority as top-down. Gibson concluded by using the words of Philip H. Coombs of the Ford Foundation to support his innovative stance: "[E]ducation is 'an undynamic, unprogressive industry,' unwilling to challenge its traditional assumptions." "Assumptions about class size are certainly a case in point," Gibson ends, extending Coombs's economic metaphor to dub his idea "profitable." By "unprogressive," Gibson seems to mean simply "unwilling to change." Raising class size so that teachers increase their hierarchical distance from their students is not progressive in the framework of the progressive education movement.

Collaborative practice in the Cold War era is interesting precisely because it exemplifies the practice of collaboration within a cultural climate antithetical to the values of American pragmatism. As much of the discussion has shown, during this period rationales other than pragmatism were drawn upon to justify collaborative pedagogy. The period is also instructive in illustrating many of the problems and contradictions that may arise when collaborative pedagogy is divorced from pragmatist assumptions. However, the situation was soon to shift with the successful collective movements of Civil Rights activism and Vietnam War protest.

3

The Era of Civil Rights and the Vietnam War

> Now we are living in a great series of revolutions, testing whether
> the present forms of school, church, state, family, and relation-
> ships between blacks and whites will endure. Already high school
> students are following the lead of college students—publishing
> underground newspapers, asking for a voice in making the rules
> of their schools. Tomorrow they will be suggesting or forcing
> changes in the classroom—in what they are asked to read, to
> write, and in how their work is to be evaluated.
>
> —Ken Macrorie, "To Be Read" (1968)

COLLABORATIVE PEDAGOGIES FLOURISHED IN THE WAKE of the
Civil Rights Movement and the Vietnam War protests. Interest in
Dewey was reconstituted in an era—much like Dewey's post–Civil
War era—in which definitions of democracy were vying for dominance, and political action was considered by a vocal minority to
be crucial to good citizenship. In this chapter I discuss two groups
of collaborative pedagogies that I call "antiestablishment pedagogy"
and "writing support pedagogy." In the former, teacher authority
was radically decentered without a blueprint for student behavior.
In the latter, student behavior was prescribed, and the teacher facilitated a focus on one student essay at a time.

"Antiestablishment pedagogy" describes a group of experimental
practices individually developed by progressive teachers who were
themselves involved in political protests. They were mostly young,
white, male assistant professors, part of a generation of scholars
hired to teach the increased population of students that the 1950s
faculty had been expecting. These antiestablishment teachers influenced their students by rebelling against authoritarian education in

the climate of Vietnam War protests on campuses. A quieter sort of rebellion characterized the creators of writing support groups, in which teachers focused on the writer's individual voice, modifying the more critical creative writing workshop by inviting gentle, positive response from the class. Support-group pedagogy was influenced by Rogerian psychology. This pedagogy could be seen as anticonflictual and supportive of peaceful solutions in the traditions of Peter Elbow (*Writing without Teachers*) and Mary Rose O'Reilley (*The Peaceable Classroom*).

Both pedagogies can be seen as responding to the political climate, as well as influencing it to some degree. Their contrasts with the antiprogressive, conformist practices of the 1950s Oregon Plan are compelling. That they take place in the context of war, antiracist activism, and a revival of interest in Dewey is interesting in light of the argument I make for collaborative learning in this book. The vitality and political promise of collaborative learning lies in its relation to its historical consciousness and the progressive principles of Dewey's intent that education can be a means for the continual renewal of US democracy. Though neither antiestablishment pedagogy nor writing support groups fully support Dewey's political goals for critical education, they do give us insight into the various roads that progressive pedagogies may take that perhaps unconsciously constrain radical impulses within the boundaries of the classroom, which was not Dewey's goal, nor mine.

Having been trained by Bruffee in the early 1980s, I am drawn to group work in which social relations are structured with clear roles for the teacher and the students toward the specific end of intellectual development and collective authority. In Bruffee's experience, students gain a sense of collective authority if given the right tasks. He didn't *give* us authority in the Summer Institute. We *took* it. His was an authoritative presence, in that he didn't try to become a member of the group. He designed tasks, put us in groups to accomplish them, left the room as a gesture toward our independence from him, then came back to keep time. When we reported to the class as a whole, he facilitated the discussion, and often presented a professional perspective from what he described as a "community of knowledgeable peers." He discussed the process of knowledge creation that had led to a "professional" interpretation of a poem, for instance. This step in the process keeps unsubstantiated pluralism at bay. We can embrace a collaboration that provides an explanation of how our interpretation may be more valid than their perhaps implausible one. John Trimbur, as a Marxist scholar, expanded this discussion to the economic means of the production of texts, which opens an opportunity to critique the profession, the culture, and capitalism.

The teacher's job was to carefully design the collaborative task so that the groups could function on their own. We negotiated the task, reported to the class, and learned about difference in this way: we saw how we interpreted the task differently than did our peers in other groups. Then the groups, led by Bruffee, negotiated with one another, and in the end we understood more about the issues involved in the task than we would have if Ken had lectured to us. Bruffee was well known in the profession. Many of us, including John Trimbur, didn't yet have PhDs. But soon we had gained enough collective authority to confront Bruffee. We had a list of demands. Social psychologist Alex Gitterman helped us through that (see his article "Collaborative Learning and Teaching" in Kail's special issue). He met with us twice a week to frame what we were going through in terms of "intimacy versus authority" and the reciprocal relationship between the individual and the group (see Bennis and Shepard).

When I read Dewey's *Experience and Education* I found my experiences confirmed. Dewey had written the book specifically to warn teachers away from "structureless" classes in which teachers decentered or "shared" their authority and students were ostensibly free. He believed that teachers should use their authority to teach democratic skills by designing tasks that students can accomplish with one another's help. Dewey did not mean for classrooms to be democracies, but rather to teach students the skills of democracy in a particular historical context, which was for him at that time the Great Depression.

In the rest of this chapter, I will address the particular historical situation of antiestablishment pedagogy and the writing support group. Then I will present the practices themselves as published in a special issue of *College English* in 1971, along with Bruffee's published response in the next issue. Antiestablishment pedagogy was creative and rebellious. Teachers were experimenting with ways of radically changing the authority of knowledge in the classroom. They stimulated students' imaginations about what was possible when established classroom behavior was turned on its head. More anarchic than constructive, it reflected a revolutionary moment in the 1960s. From Dewey's 1930s perspective, however, it was more of a reaction to the political environment than a training ground for political effectiveness. Its failure to thrive was productive nevertheless. The system would be broken before it could be reconstructed. And Bruffee was a major part of the reconstruction. Support group pedagogy was also rebellious in its quiet way. It replaced attention to grammatical correctness with the rhetoric of ethos. Although support group pedagogy supported the individual's voice, which was a crucial part of democracy for Dewey, it looked inward, privileging the individual's psyche over the world outside.

CULTURAL CONTEXT

Antiracist and antiwar protests, similar to the populist movements in the 1930s, contributed to an educational environment that supported collaborative learning. This environment, ironically, was initially propelled with funding made available because of the Cold War. In response to the USSR's launching of Sputnik in October 1957, Congress passed the National Defense Education Act (NDEA) in 1958. In the same year the Ford Foundation funded the 1958 Basic Issues Conference to define English studies, against progressive education, as a "fundamental liberal discipline" conceived as "a core of experience, a body of knowledge, and a set of specific skills to be attained" (qtd. in Harris, "After Dartmouth" 636). In 1961, spurred by NCTE lobbying and the publication of its dramatic report, *The National Interest and the Teaching of English,*[14] English studies was funded by the NDEA under the name of Project English, and the project's declaration of purpose was published in both *College English* and *College Composition and Communication* in 1962.[15] Project English helped initiate a liaison between university and high school teachers, leading to the 1966 Dartmouth Seminar, a three-week meeting sponsored by the MLA, NCTE, and NATE and funded by the Carnegie Corporation. The move toward federal funding of education for national defense purposes was partly responsible for the growth of rhetoric in the university setting in the subsequent years.

Brown v. Board of Education (1954) and the court actions that followed further strengthened the role of the federal government in education. The effective and highly visible tactics of the Civil Rights Movement merged into the later protest of the Vietnam War by students on college campuses around the country. This turbulent era, with its conflicting ideologies, was reflected in English departments in new ways of approaching literature and rhetoric, among them Marxist, expressive (reader response), and socially based literary criticism and rhetoric.

One of the first hints we see of a shift in *College English* is Richard Ohmann's "In Lieu of a New Rhetoric," published in 1964. This article indicates a turning point from conservative cold war "factism" toward academic acceptance of a diversified approach to rhetoric. Ohmann begins the article by noting the ambiguous meaning of "rhetoric" in current usage. "We have here," he writes, "one of those infinitely expandable and contractible notions—such as 'democracy' and 'virtue'—that can be suited to the exigencies of the moment" (18). Ohmann then describes some underlying similarities in the various new rhetorics. Instead of constraining a new rhetoric by prematurely restricting it to a tight definition, Ohmann seeks to maintain—in a Burkean fashion—a multiplicity of views on the subject. This position, furthermore, is theoretically grounded in one of the major consensual claims of the new rhetoric itself: truth emerges from the process of discourse.

Ohmann became editor of *College English* in 1966 and significantly influenced the field for fourteen years. Just as he had advocated a variety of voices in his 1964 article, he supported a variety of social, leftist, minority, and anarchist positions in the journal. Ohmann devoted special issues to Marxist literature, gay and lesbian themes, and antiestablishment pedagogy, giving control of one issue to two graduate students who published articles written only by students. His editorship reflected the open-mindedness of both the man and the era, and as a result the journal portrays the extremes of the period, exemplified by the "Comment and Rebuttal" section that Ohmann instituted. Ohmann's approach to rhetoric and education and his editorial position reflected the attitudes of many faculty at the time who believed in the social and personal relevance of education.

Consistent with Ohmann's notion of diverse rhetorics, Mina Shaughnessy's *Errors and Expectations* attempted to explain the linguistic patterns of the sudden influx of economically and culturally diverse students into the City University of New York system with the advent of open admissions in the summer of 1970. She introduced into the field the term *basic writer*, which from a twenty-first-century perspective is problematic in its unconscious denigration of Black English Vernacular (BEV). On the other hand, she is one of the few leaders in the field at that time who focused specifically on the needs of the students for whom admissions were opened. The landmark CCCC position statement *Students' Right to Their Own Language* (1974) was spearheaded by Geneva Smitherman, linguist James Sledd, and others who responded to the needs of the new population of students.

Against this background of social protest and change emerged a variety of "self-actualizing" psychologies. This was in part due to the influence of Carl Rogers and the popularization of therapy groups.[16] Rogers supported the use of groups on the condition that they be nonevaluative and assist the individual in self-validation. With these supportive characteristics, according to Rogers, groups provide a milieu in which the individual may sensitively, without fear of rejection or reprisal, explore and discover him- or herself. In fact, in a climate of group trust, the individual may actually be encouraged to be more him- or herself.

Rogerian psychology was appealing to many educators during the seventies, and its influence continues. Unlike the then-predominant experimental, research-based psychology that was concerned primarily with identifying the elemental characteristics of human behavior (running rats through mazes), humanistic psychology such as Rogers's was interested in the individual human being. As such it struck a responsive chord among educators concerned with their students. Rogers supported educators' using his methods in their classrooms.[17] In a number of his writings he equated education and therapy, much as Dewey had earlier equated education and philosophy.

The Rogerian paradigm in English education was given a substantial boost by the Dartmouth Seminar in 1966, at which teachers and scholars from the United States and Great Britain met at Dartmouth College to discuss the teaching of English in the public schools (Berlin, *Rhetoric and Reality* 149; Harris, "After Dartmouth"). Arthur Applebee has noted that the British contribution to American pedagogy at the conference was an emphasis on student-centered teaching, a contribution that supported the reemergence of a progressive agenda.

ANTIESTABLISHMENT PEDAGOGY

At 10:48 p.m., April 3, 1969, I watched the president of my university leave his mansion and, followed by about thirty white-helmeted policemen carrying clubs and marching in tight formation behind him, stride across the street and up the walk of the Student Union to clear out any students who insisted on sitting in the Snack Bar after the eleven o'clock closing hour.

I had been a professor more than twenty years. The sight was new, and it made me sick.

Not because the president was acting irrationally.

Not because the students were acting irrationally.

But because the professors were not there. In the last five years I had learned something about their responsibility in this affair. More than anyone else, they have made the university sick unto death.

—Ken Macrorie, "Prologue," *Uptaught* (1970)

Antiestablishment pedagogy, with its defining characteristic of un-directed rebellion, was prevalent in *College English* from 1967 to 1973. Although diverse, approaches of the era shared similar attitudes toward authority, knowledge, and social relations, distinguishing them sharply from the collaborative learning of the Cold War. The 1950s sense of knowledge as scientific and objective, authority as respectable, and social relations as suspect were radically changed in collaborative practice so that knowledge and authority were suspect and egalitarian social relations were privileged.

The overriding issue is authority. Teachers who write about collaborative practice in antiestablishment pedagogy attempt to relinquish their institutional authority as much as possible; they want to empower their students *as individuals*. Harvey Stuart Irlen's attitude is representative. In "Toward Confronting Freshmen" (1970), he proposes to tear down the walls between teachers and students by paying more serious attention to students' needs. "The freshman is a person," Irlen writes, "and I must be free enough to deal with him, to communicate with him, to teach him, as an individual" (36). In describing his role as a "consultant," Robert Sutherland ("Letting Students Be: Report on a Continuing Experiment in Education," 1971, 738) says that he supports his students in pursuing their own individual initiatives in whatever way is best for them, either in or out of class.

This kind of freedom, proponents of antiestablishment pedagogy noted, demands student engagement and responsibility. Sutherland echoes Dewey when he states: "If learning—and education—is to be maximally achieved, the student must feel that he has a real stake in the way his learning is taking place" (735). Sutherland and Irlen are representative in their concern that students participate in course planning. Sutherland's students served as members of "class councils" of five or six students, membership in which rotated throughout the term so that all class members served, working with the teacher on evaluating the class activities, planning, both long-term and short-term, and maintaining a sense of community in the class as a whole. Irlen discusses this theme informally, saying that students should have a say in the subject matter as well as the structure of the course. This exacts a wholehearted commitment from both teacher and student. "The instructor cannot do all the work," says Irlen, "and the student can function more vitally than a parrot" (38).

There is a strong sense of egalitarianism in these articles, not just between the teacher and the student, but among students as well. Echoing the discourse of integration brought by *Brown v. Board of Education* (1954), Irlen says that the most important priority is that students not be divided according to intellectual ability or economic or cultural background (37). Using the language of US democratic governance when speaking of his "class council," Sutherland says: "Members serving the council are in no sense an elite group, but rather the representatives of the rest of the class, whom they regard as constituents to be served" (737). This is particularly interesting in regard to the prevalence of ability grouping in both the 1920s and the 1950s, and it was an appropriate change in the wake of civil rights activism.

The characteristic attempt to shift authority to the individual student is accompanied with a rejection of "scientific" or objective knowledge. Sutherland asked his students to grade themselves, contending that the practice would be educative and supportive of an atmosphere of community. Irlen proposed a pass/fail system, with the rationale that "[p]laying the game for grades is insidious enough in any course. In a composition course it is disastrous" (38–39). It is disastrous, according to Irlen, because it neglects to engage the unique needs and interests of each student, and because it supports an "objective" view of knowledge.

Sutherland follows Irlen in contending that in composition it is ridiculous to talk about grades because there is no such thing as a "right" or "wrong" answer. "I do not grade examinations," Sutherland notes, "but instead make critical comments which are addressed to the student as an individual" (737). He adds that often he asks the students to make up their own tests. H. R. Wolf from SUNY Buffalo, whose article "The Classroom as Microcosm" is one of a cluster titled "Personal Teaching: A Discussion" (1971), describes his class as based on methods of group therapy and confesses his past misguided assumptions of "literature as a neutral methodology" and "the classroom as a clearing house where information and concepts were brokered from one person to a set of others" (260). Gary Margolis, whose article "Taking It All Off: Teaching in the Therapeutic Classroom," is a response to Wolf's, states flatly: "Science is on the outs with most students, especially the way it works and what we have let it do to us" (281).[18]

This is a distinctive turn from the 1950s' unquestioning obeisance to the authority of the teacher and a spectator epistemology, which had impoverished collaborative pedagogy during the Cold War. The dominant assumptions of 1960s and 1970s collaboration are, rather, reminiscent of the prevailing assumptions of the 1930s, during which there was a similar climate of social unrest and the hope (in some quarters) for change in the political order. Whereas many articles in the 1930s exhibited a roughly pragmatist epistemology, however, the dominant articles of the protest era reflect a notion of knowledge as radically subjective.

Knowledge in this group of articles is conceived of as an "inner" experience that can be released or "discovered" under the right conditions. Teachers should provide the kind of atmosphere that allows students' true selves to surface: this should definitely not be the kind of atmosphere in which the student must seek the teacher's approval (Sutherland 734). In describing what was wrong with his early teaching experience, Wolf says that the students' writing did not become "precise and personalized, accurate and clear in the only sense that is important: the unique expression of one's unique experience" ("Composition and Group Dynamics" 441). In describing the strengths of one of his later teaching experiences, Wolf clearly privileges the personal over the social: "Almost all of our meetings were intense and fruitful; and they continued to be person-centered rather than interactional" ("Classroom" 265). The focus on student-centered activities rather than teacher-centered lectures qualifies antiestablishment pedagogy as collaborative practice, but the privileging of the minds of individual students contrasts with both Dewey's emphasis and the social-constructionist practice that would follow.

This focus on the student, rather than on authoritative knowledge, led to the breakdown of the conventional boundaries of subject matter in these classes. In his "Classroom as Microcosm" essay Wolf describes how he jettisoned the reading list for his course on the "Literature of Mental Crisis and Madness" (Freud, Jung, Gogol, and Dostoyevsky) after he perceived hostility from his students. Wolf asked the class members to discuss their feelings, "making it clear that I, in no way, construed the expression of hostility towards the course or instructor as unnatural." The discussion ended with Wolf abandoning all the course materials and changing the subject of the course to "*the group itself*" (261). Students submitted anonymous accounts of personal crises, which served as the subject matter of the course. Along with innovation in subject matter came an emphasis on education as process. The process, as was true of some collaborative learning in the 1930s, was often "evolutionary," in the sense that the course was not necessarily structured ahead of time by the teacher. "There is no such thing as structured creativity," states Irlen.[19] "Perhaps a course that deals with structured creativity can be graded. A course that chooses to deal with students cannot be" (37, 39).

Showing similarities to Dewey's pragmatist concerns, antiestablishment scholarship frames itself within the context of contemporary political issues. Irlen begins his article with this statement:

> I am suggesting that teachers, including the teachers of freshman composition, have allowed the very structures of their courses to come between them and their students, and so to hamper education by reflecting the same kind of polarity, on a smaller scale, that we deplore in our society at large. (35)

Some collaborative pedagogy during this period is self-consciously revolutionary, in deliberate response to the social protest that was going on outside the classroom. Other teachers looked at collaboration as a peaceful alternative to violent student protest. Margolis concludes his article by saying "A national, community, or family mental health begins with good, one-to-one relationships" (282). In response to the complicated political situation of the university

Wolf hopes "that *individual* teachers and departments can begin to advance new educational concepts of human development and conflict-resolution" ("Classroom" 260).

The most striking form of antiestablishment pedagogy was centered on the contemporary art form called the "Happening." The Happening attempts to tear down institutional authority as completely as possible (and thus stimulate creativity) through the use of shock, surprise, chaos, and spontaneity. Geoffrey Sirc explores the relationship between the art form and the composition class, noting that

> [s]o many of the happening tenets come directly from Duchamp—the notion of art as art-in-general, as conceptual; the emphasis on language; the use of objects not produced by the artist (the readymade); chance as compositional strategy; the anti-institutional stance; the disinclination to discuss meaning, and the importance of the viewer as originator of art's meaning.[20] ("English" 288)

The first of the articles discussing these ideas appeared in *College English* in 1967, aptly titled "English Composition as a Happening," by Charles Deemer, a postgraduate student novelist from Oregon. Like Macrorie's *Uptaught,* Deemer's article represents a rebellion in form. It is a series of discursive comments by the author alternating with long quotations from contemporary cult figures such as Marshall McLuhan, John Dewey, and Susan Sontag. These prose pieces are separated from one another by horizontal sets of three large dots and lapses of conceptual coherence. Deemer suggests that the teacher get rid of the podium and stand at the back of the room, or possibly outside the window, and "discuss theology to Ray Charles records." The student should never be "corrected" by the teacher. "With this," warns Deemer, "authority returns." Deemer apologizes for the confusion that might result from his lack of explicitness about how to produce a Happening. "Spontaneity is essential," he explains (124). William Lutz, who in 1971 published "Making Freshman English a Happening," suggests seating students in a circle, turning off the lights, and having a discussion.

Lutz asked his students to write about the experience afterwards. Lutz called the Happening "a structure in unstructure; a random series of ordered events; order in chaos; the logical illogicality of dreams." The Happening, according to Lutz, "calls for the complete restructuring of the university" (35).

As in the art form, the purpose of the Happening is defamiliarization, to introduce students to an experience they haven't had before, to make them aware that there are ways of viewing the world that they haven't experienced. This could stimulate creative thinking. According to Sirc, two prominent innovators of Happening pedagogy in the late 1960s were Ken Macrorie and W. E. Coles. *Uptaught,* which begins with the inscription at the beginning of this section, reads like a collage. Sirc describes Macrorie's *Uptaught* as

> a panic-text, apocalyptically reading the scene of instructional theory in writing against the crisis-moment of the late 1960s. He reacted precisely against the metaphysics of the code he saw working itself out in his students, causing them to produce "mechanical exercises . . . all dead" (6); he tried to trace our way back to a truthful idiom. ("English" 280)

Coles's pedagogy is more nuanced. In "The Sense of Nonsense as a Design for Sequential Writing Assignments," Coles describes his method as using language to have students experience identity shifts through the disruption of the language they use. Citing the example of "Jabberwocky," Coles uses spatial metaphors to articulate a design very similar to art Happenings. "Nonsense," he notes, "consists of a peculiar fusion of pattern and anti-pattern, of ordered disorder" (28). Coles's sophisticated assignments for the topic of rebellion and conformity in one of his classes begin with the question: "What does it mean to change your mind?" (29).

Although antiestablishment pedagogy took place in a culture of successful collective action, the pedagogy itself focused on individual change. This perhaps is a reaction to 1950s conformity, which stifled individual creativity and often viewed individual difference with suspicion. This was an animating conflict in the culture—

collective political action versus spiritual actualization. Just as the art version of the Happening successfully resisted fetishization and commodification, so did antiestablishment pedagogy resist institutionalization. The key animating political feature of these antiestablishment pedagogues appears to have been general opposition to the constricting character of the social system.

Critique

Critiques of antiestablishment pedagogy covered the political spectrum, focusing on issues of authority, the individualistic concept of the student self—reminiscent of some 1930s collaborative pedagogy—and the relationship of the collaborative schemes to political issues. Other critics found this pedagogy simply impractical. Granville Jones, director of the first-year English course called "The Literary Imagination" at Carnegie-Mellon University, described in the December 1971 issue of *College English* his experimental course using student-directed methods. Jones left his course completely up to the students. In his first attempt at the course, he attended class twice during the semester; in his second attempt, he attended class all but the last three weeks. Jones describes his experiment as a failure, citing instances of student apathy and their inability to structure the course and lead discussions. In describing the failure of their attempts to get students to lead the discussions of literature, one of Jones's students remarked perceptively: "We had returned to the teacher figure—only ours was less prepared to do the job" (289). Another student, drawing on his recent classroom experience with *Paradise Lost,* blamed Jones: "I feel that it was your *responsibility* to see that we didn't fail. You should have prevented it rather than allow it. It was wrong to play both God (inevitable being teacher) and devil" (293). It is perhaps fair to infer from Jones's concluding remarks that he may not have listened carefully to his students:

> Convinced that *we* have learned a lot but that each subsequent class seems destined to repeat the mistakes of preceding ones, we have decided that a student-directed course is a lovely idea that simply will not work. The freer the group, the more unreliable the performance; the more controlled the group, the less legitimate the label student-directed. (293)

Jones may have been caught in the framework of the traditional, authoritarian classroom. Seeing the teacher's authority as all or nothing, his image of student authority could have been a reflection of his conventional notions of teacher authority.

Raymond Bentman of Temple University responded to Jones's article in the "Comment and Rebuttal" section of *College English*. Bentman noted that Jones was guilty of the assumption commonly held by critics of innovative teaching methods—"that conventional higher education is delightfully successful so that any new practice must compare favorably to an ideal" (462). We do not notice problems in conventional courses as readily, Bentman contended, because we are used to them. Responding to Jones's comment that a peer-taught class he visited was "the dullest forty-five minutes I have ever sat through," Bentman claimed that he had both sat through and taught plenty of dull conventional classes at such eminent domiciles of higher learning as the University of Pennsylvania and Yale (462). Bentman concluded by contending that collaborative classes should not be judged within the same (unquestioned) assumptions of conventional teaching (464).[21]

Wilson Currin Snipes, in a somewhat less dramatic failure of a student-directed course, began his experiment at Virginia Polytechnic Institute and State University with a similar set of expectations about authority as had Jones. His article "An Inquiry: Peer Group Teaching in Freshman Writing," begins with a set of assumptions: that writing is central, that it must be read by a "competent reader," that "the integrity of the student's experience with a work of art" is primary, and that "the student must be given an opportunity, usually through written and oral expression, to express, analyze, interpret, and evaluate these experiences; to do so under competent instruction, an opportunity for discussion and performance must be provided each student." His central question was "[C]an freshman students teach one another to write effectively?" (170). The teacher planned everything scrupulously, but presented it as a series of suggestions to the class members, who were responsible for running the class (171). What happened, according to Snipes, was as expected: some students participated and some did not (172). Students cited as advantages the opportunity for independent thought, informality, shared responsibility, and exposure to a multiplicity of perspectives. Students' complaints centered on the issue of authority, including poor teaching by the students, the lack of experience students had in taking control of their own learning, and the discrepancy between the teachers' responsibility to evaluate and grade, and the students' responsibility to teach (173). It is hardly surprising that, left to their own devices in a classroom, students would feel the need to create an authority figure in the image of their teacher. It is surprising, however, that Snipes, who appears to have been genuinely interested in innovative teaching, did not question that image of authority and offer an alternative model. As I discuss in the introduction to this chapter, Dewey had warned against the dangers of this kind of abdication of teacher authority in 1932 in *Experience and Education.*

Kenneth Bruffee's critique most fully comprehends the problem with authority in many of the protest classrooms. Richard Ohmann asked Bruffee to respond to the December 1971 special issue of *College English*, which he did in a piece called "The Way Out: A Critical Survey of Innovations in College Teaching, with Special Reference to the December, 1971, Issue of *College English*," published in January 1972. The article is a critique of the implications for authority of the social relationships (among students and between students and teacher) advocated by antiestablishment pedagogy (458). For teaching to be truly innovative, Bruffee argues, it must actively support an alternative kind of authority engendered by collaborative relationships among students. Rather than leave students alone (as did Jones and Snipes) or collaborate with students (as did Wolf) or disorient students (as in the Happening), Bruffee maintains that the traditional classroom relationships must be "actively disrupted" and replaced with an alternate structure (461). Bruffee replaces Wolf's notion of decentralization with polycentralization. "The basic pattern of centralization," Bruffee explains,

> is the strong individual contending with other weaker, isolated, usually hierarchically organized individuals. The basic pattern of polycentralization is a number of small groups more or less equal in power contending with one another.

Each group supports individuals working collaboratively with other individuals in it, and thereby increases the power of each individual to equal the power of the group as a whole. (461–62)

Bruffee notes that the success of student activism proves that students know how to organize themselves collectively under the right conditions.[22] The students' vast experience in traditional learning, however, has ill prepared them for collaborative behavior in the classroom. Bruffee notes that the value of Jones's experiments with student-directed teaching is that it gives us an empirical description of the passivity "a lifetime of traditional learning" has engendered in our students.

Bruffee's next move is to attack the independent, individualist notion of the student subject assumed by the majority of the protest teachers. Bruffee questions the validity, for instance, of trying to find one's true self by shedding the need for others' approval:

Is it not true that it is only in infancy (and in our infantile moments as adults) that we are concerned exclusively to please ourselves? When we work maturely and at our best, do we not work to please those we want to please, which usually, but seldom exclusively, includes ourselves? Does our proper self-evaluation as adults not depend to a considerable extent on the success of our attempts to serve others, as well as ourselves? Is the desire to please others necessarily equivalent to the desire to please "superiors," that is, people with power to break us? (464–65)

Bruffee's argument implies that an individualist concept of self-expression is not conducive to collaborative learning (or life experiences). Teachers (such as Wolf) who think of individual initiative as the highest good are sabotaging their own efforts at promoting collaboration in their classrooms. Bruffee reserves his praise for that collaborative practice which encourages students to make genuine and purposeful connections with other students and with the larger world. The tension Bruffee points out in antiestablishment pedagogy harks back to the social expressive tension of 1930s collaborative learning.

In this respect, Bruffee's critique is similar to Brent Harold's leftist response, "Beyond Student-Centered Teaching: The Dialectical Materialist Form of a Literature Course" (1972). Harold attacks antiestablishment pedagogy for its idealism, by which he means "the tendency to experience ideas as abstracted from the concrete, social experiences of the people holding them, as well as to abstract the people themselves from their actual classroom and other social situations" (201). Harold cites as one of his examples of this idealism the class as pseudocollective. This refers to the student's belief that he is not responsible for the success or failure of the class, that it is "something happening to him." With Bruffee, Harold contends that students believe this because they normally do not have any real work to do together in such classes (203). Harold's critique moves beyond the scope of Bruffee's piece in his attack on education without advocacy. Education ought to encourage students to develop their own stances, rather than to "[accumulate] . . . stances," writes Harold (202). He argues that the essay is a context in which the student can do this. Harold suggests that innovative teaching should involve students in relating their own social and economic experience to the social and economic experience reflected in the work of literature they are studying. Both Bruffee and Harold criticize antiestablishment pedagogy for its neglect of a coherent theory (as opposed to blind faith). Each of them asserts the necessity of rigorously thinking through the nature of classroom social roles and expectations and the linkage between the classroom and the broader society.

WRITING SUPPORT GROUPS

We believe teachers must learn to sit down and shut up.
—Lou Kelly, "Toward Competence and
Creativity in an Open Class" (1973)

Practitioners of writing support groups taught a benevolent version of the creative writing workshop in which the group was support for the writer. The purpose of the 1970s writing support groups is to help the individual find his or her "voice." Writing is perceived as an individual process based on spontaneity and originality. Some advocates have explicit connections to creative writing. Donald Murray was a professional writer and journalist. Both Betty Shiflett and John Schultz (the originator of the Story Workshop method) were novelists. And Lou Kelly spoke from the University of Iowa, best known for its Writers' Workshop. The authors of many of these articles borrow their techniques from the writing of poetry, fiction, and journalistic prose.

A basic assumption of these writing groups is that writing cannot be taught. S. I. Hayakawa addresses this issue in the conclusion of his 1962 article "Learning to Think and Write: Semantics in Freshman English":

> How, then, shall writing be taught? I am just about coming to the conclusion that it should not be taught at all. I believe that instruction in grammar, spelling, sentence structure, paragraphing and such should be abandoned in Freshman English. The students should be told that the lid is off, that they can write and spell and punctuate any damn way they please—but that they must write daily and copiously. (8)

Hayakawa assumes that what teachers normally teach in the classroom about writing is a hindrance to students, who need freedom in order to release what is inside them. Lou Kelly ends her 1973 article on a similar note. Not only is writing unteachable, asserts Kelly, but the teaching of writing is unteachable as well. The writing group leader relies on personal experience (660). In Shiflett's article on the Story Workshop this principle is emphasized once more: The "discovery process cannot be accomplished by any amount of explaining or defining *for* the student what the discovery *ought* to be" (149).

Writing as conceptualized in this group of articles is unquestionably a process of discovery. There is near-consensus on four issues: the importance of freewriting, of students' talking with one another about their work, of putting grammar and mechanics last, and of "publishing." It is interesting to note the point-by-point parallel between these beliefs and key assumptions of Rogerian psychology. The importance of freewriting and putting mechanics last is closely related to the Rogerian emphasis on the importance of the client's talk and a noninhibiting environment, exemplified in the nonevaluative stance of the therapist. The issue of students' talking with each other parallels Roger's notion of sharing, while the necessity of "publishing" students' writing corresponds to the Rogerian dictum that it is necessary to symbolize aspects of oneself in order to truly recognize and own them.

In a pedagogy in which writing cannot be taught, what then is the role of the teacher? The teacher takes various roles in these articles: all are a departure from the lecture model. In Thom Hawkins's "Group Inquiry Techniques for Teaching Writing" (1976), students are divided into permanent groups of five members each; the groups have an administrative structure (chair, timekeeper, etc.) that makes it possible for them to review the members' papers and make suggestions for improvement consistently throughout the semester. Within this framework, Hawkins says, "the teacher becomes a floating resource, assisting but not directing discussion. In a sense the teacher becomes a student" (637). The theme of teacher as learner is also explicit in Kelly's description of the open classroom. Kelly's class is a required tutorial in the writing lab, which she conducts by putting students in groups. She loosens the boundary between learning and teaching, stating that "the teacher also learns and each learner also teaches." The teacher is a group member, a resource person, an editor, but never solely an authority figure. Kelly paraphrases a key Rogerian tenet when she asserts, "We believe teachers must learn to sit down and shut up" (648). Avoiding the authority-figure role, however, requires constant vigilance, as indicated by Kelly's revealing remark: "[W]e are always trying *not* to dominate everything that happens" (649).

Donald Murray encourages a more active role for the teacher.[23] Murray describes a procedure in which the central interaction is between student and teacher. Peer response is the last step, when the student "publishes" his or her paper for an audience. Murray's teacher, in journalistic style, has four responsibilities: to enforce deadlines, to "cultivate a climate of failure," to diagnose problems (rather than "correct" them), and to create an appropriate psychological and physical environment (in this case, Murray's writing lab, equipped with typewriters) ("Finding Your Own Voice" 121–22). More subtly powerful than Murray's image of teacher, however, is the teacher described in Shiflett's "Story Workshop as a Method of Teaching Writing."[24] In this method, in which there is a great emphasis on seeing, telling, and reading, as well as writing, the group members sit around the director in a semicircle:

> The director is a power in the semi-circle and should never experience himself otherwise. He should simply place full concentration on the strengthening aspects of that power. It is largely through his sensitive use of approval, voice, gesture, and selection that the student apprehends the positive, often stringent, demands necessary for his process and growth. (151)

When the student is allowed to sit in the director's chair, according to Shiflett, "it brings added clarity and authority to his readings" (152). Much is made in this article about the responsible use of the director's approval. The director is expected on the one hand not to reveal any biases by the smallest nod or glance so the student is not led to please him or her. On the other hand,

> [h]e may rightly express his approval of the quality of perception in the writing itself. When the director finds himself inclined to give approval to any form of sentimentality, or to writing that tries for the stereotyped laugh, the joke, or the punch line, or to writings that are notable mainly for their *avoidance* of perception, then both he and the workshop are in trouble. (150)

This assumes a standard of quality that is perceived by both the author and his or her community and discovered by the student in the workshop. Even though the writing valued in this genre is described as spontaneous and original, it is expected to strike a resonant chord in the other members of the group.

This leads me to the focus of this kind of writing group—finding a voice. In describing a week in which his students conducted class during his absence, Hawkins reveals: "Many of them found their voices that week, and the following papers were greatly improved" (644). The Story Workshop method is based on the theory that the discovery of one's voice will lead to the gaining of originality, most often through the use of the senses, particularly sight and hearing. Shiflett suggests to her students that they read their papers aloud in order to make the connection between their spoken and written voices (149). Teachers of these writing groups, above all, want to be surprised. The problem with familiar words and phrases is that they are conventional. The goal is originality.

What, then, is the reason for the group, if not to help students learn the nature of convention? For Hayakawa it is therapy. He compares the first-year writing class with group therapy in that

> a relaxed and permissive atmosphere is desirable, because one acquires self-insight not by being pushed and harassed (and the teacher's red pencil is a form of harassment), but by being encouraged to try out one's ideas in discussions or written themes in an environment free of the fear of censure. (7)

For Murray, the group is an earned audience for the students, one they have to please if their work is to be successful. Kelly's group is a "community of learners" (654), "a means for releasing more talk, from everybody, and for giving each person maximum feedback on the ideas he expresses" (651). Shiflett makes it clear that the aim of the Story Workshop method is to provide a supportive milieu in which one's unique voice can be found. "What helps the individual," she continues, "is good for the group effort" (148). For writing-support-group advocates, the authority rests with the individuals' discovery of their voices. By giving sympathetic encouragement the group can help one another shed their inhibitions and get in touch with themselves. The group can also provide a necessary critical eye, to let writers know if they are relying on convention instead of their own voices.

The strengths of support-group pedagogy lie in its motivation for students to write. Coming from the 1950s conception of teaching writing as correcting errors, this is an enormous contribution, particularly in the healing of writing anxiety. Its focus on support, rather than on interaction or persuasion, motivates students, but, according to its critics, truncates their already limited social consciousness. Jeffrey Youdelman (in a somewhat different context) writes: "Already stuck in a world of daily detail, with limited horizons and stunted consciousness, students are forced deeper into their solipsistic prisons" (564). The debate over the privileging of the individual or the social is a continual productive tension in collaborative learning.

In 1964, Ohmann presaged the multiplicity of rhetorics that were to come, and to some extent used his power as *College English* editor to make it happen. Rooted in a social materialist attentiveness, Ohmann had tapped into groundbreaking collective movements, and he helped bring that attentiveness to composition studies. Teachers in the late 1960s and 1970s were members of the antiwar generation, and they brought that sense of rebellion into their pedagogy, both influencing and supporting their students' collective and individual forms of protest. The three major figures who in some sense drew from these currents were Peter Elbow, Kenneth Bruffee, and Ira Shor, to whom I devote the following chapter. A less prominent but no less significant contribution to the history of collaborative pedagogy comes from scholars on race and racism.

4

Elbow, Bruffee, Shor, and Antiracist Pedagogy

> The way you describe your own difficulties organizing collab-
> orative learning suggests to me that you may have been going
> about it, from my point of view, backwards. "It seemed to me
> I'd taught ineptly," you say, when "I'd relinquished substantial
> authority and yet students hadn't ended up with any more. Per-
> haps less" (p. 8n). To me it seems that to "relinquish" authority is
> just another way of maintaining control of it. . . . Collaborative
> learning helps members of the learning group invest authority in
> each other, so that they gain the capacity to divest the leader of
> some of his or her authority.
>
> —Kenneth Bruffee, letter to Peter Elbow (1981)

CHAPTER 3 PROVIDED THE GROUNDWORK AND HISTORICAL rationale for antiestablishment and support-group pedagogy, versions
of which came into prominence with the work of Peter Elbow and
Kenneth Bruffee. In this chapter, I argue that although student
group work would likely have continued into the late twentieth century in some form, Elbow and Bruffee—both influenced by John
Dewey—are largely responsible for the way we think about and
practice collaborative learning today. And Dewey's legacy would be
incomplete without Ira Shor's attention to the impact of economic
class. Shor has picked up the mantle of Dewey's more radical political leanings. Furthermore, collaborative practice is embraced by
proponents of antiracist pedagogy in the field of education.

PETER ELBOW: THE LEADER OF
SUPPORT-GROUP PEDAGOGY

Peter Elbow published his first piece in *College English* in 1968. Titled "A Method for Teaching Writing," it was followed one issue later with a second article, "The Definition of Teaching." When Elbow wrote those articles he was a young teacher at the Massachusetts Institute of Technology. He had quit graduate school because of a temporary inability to write. These initial articles, Elbow has reported, were his way out of that quandary. His teaching experience had given him something he wished to say to English teachers, and *College English* gave him an audience. In his 1971 article "Exploring My Teaching," he first published his thoughts on the importance of peer-group pedagogy. His best-selling book *Writing without Teachers* (1973) established his reputation as an authority on the teacherless class. In 1981 Elbow published his nearly equally successful *Writing with Power* for individual writers. Elbow's *College English* article "Closing My Eyes as I Speak: An Argument for Ignoring Audience" represents a cyclic turning back and forth from the individual to the group that has continued to the present day. In his successful attempt to reach a broad audience and in his focus on experience and giving students voice, Elbow's work is in line with Dewey's focus on the need for a strong individual voice in democratic participation.

I turn now to a description of Elbow's group practice.[25] Elbow's "teacherless" writing group can meet with or without a teacher. If it meets with a teacher, the teacher must serve as a functioning member of the group. The group consists of seven to twelve committed people who meet once a week. Ample time should be set aside for the discussion of everyone's paper and a monitor should apportion the time equally. The writer is in control of his or her own feedback, serving as leader during the discussion of his or her piece. All the feedback for the first few weeks is positive. The writer decides when he or she wants the negative feedback to start. All feedback, even the negative feedback, should be in the form of "movies of people's minds while they read your words," as opposed to "advice about what changes to make" or "theories of what is good and bad writing" (*Writing without Teachers* 77). A writer might ask for a paraphrase of his or her paper, for positive feedback, or for reader-based (emotional response) or criterion-based (standard evaluation) feedback. No one in the group is permitted to argue with a response. Asking for clarification is acceptable. The point is to "[bring] out the *maximum* differences [within the group] but . . . not to fight things out or try to settle on the truth" (110–11). Note the dialectical nature of this method. Elbow indicates his emphasis on the individual when he says, "A functioning class exploits the differences *between* individuals to pry open more diversity *within* individuals" (115). Five minutes should be set aside at the end of each session for a group evaluation of the session itself.

It is obvious in the way his group tasks are set up that Elbow is less interested in conventional standards than in internal, affective response. Conventional standards may have kept many writers from writing at all. Elbow suggests "movies of people's minds," indicating that it is not only the internal world of the writer that is important but also the internal worlds of the peer respondents. The "no arguing" rule puts the burden of response on description, rather than on judgment. For Elbow, description and personal response are more persuasive rhetorical strategies than simple, straightforward "arguments against" the writer's choices. The writers' intentions and what they wrote and what they like about their essays are true and important and their responders' mind logs ("I am bored by this part, confused by this, excited about that") are also true and important. This can provoke reflection on the part of the writer to think more deeply about his or her take on an essay and the reader's take as well.

The stated goal of Elbow's peer feedback is for students to develop a sense of judgment about their writing (*Writing without Teachers* viii). When one's writing is the focus of discussion, he or she runs the group and controls the kind of feedback he or she gets. But the writer doesn't get to argue with a peer's response. He or she "takes in" the responses, and then makes his or her own choices (104). Elbow wants the students' sense of judgment to extend to what Nancy Schniedewind calls "group leadership." Elbow says to students, "[Y]ou must take responsibility for what happens in class: if you don't try to stop [whatever is going on], you must want it to happen" (115). In Elbow's teacherless classroom, there is no titular authority, which is part of the point.

Note this, for emphasis: the teacher is absent in Elbow's ideal collaborative class. If he or she must be there (in academic settings, for instance), the teacher becomes a member of the group. To mitigate the inevitable power relationship between the teacher and the student in an academic setting, Elbow makes ground rules (such as grading criteria and due dates for assignments) absolutely clear. Elbow writes: "I feel I can best minimize this power relationship by getting the weapons out on the table" ("Exploring" 750). Elbow further weakens the power of the teacher by warning his students (and his readers) that a teacher does not make the best audience for a student's paper. The teacher cannot respond effectively to each student's paper, but is more likely to submit student papers to standard evaluative norms (*Writing without Teachers* 127 and *Writing with Power* 216–36), which Elbow says is less effective than unmediated individual response. Elbow's writing class is subversive in that he brackets the institutional setting and encourages student writers to appropriate it for their own uses.

And for good reason. The teacher has functioned as the most critical reader for most students, often inhibiting students' ability to write. Elbow's conditions are designed to help students *want* to write—thus no negative feedback for the first few weeks. An audience can stimulate writing, but it can also prevent writing. Elbow's pedagogy almost guarantees a "safe" audience. "It's easy to know when you should start getting feedback," Elbow advises in *Writing with Power*:

> Just keep in mind what's more important than what: writing is more important than sharing your writing with readers; and sharing your writing with readers is more important than getting feedback from them. That is, if sharing begins to stop you from writing, then don't share. And if getting feedback begins to stop you from writing or sharing, then stop getting feedback. Writing is what's most important. (238)

Elbow does not suggest that writing is, at its best, a solitary enterprise. "[W]hen you can share and get feedback *without* hampering your writing," he writes, "then you will benefit enormously from those two activities" (238). Elbow defines power as "the power to make a difference" (280). He describes writing as an "act of *giving*" (20). An important part of the gift is the writer's voice, the act of "taking full responsibility for your words" (22). Elbow sees genuine voice (or "ethos") as persuasive in itself. "Real voice," says Elbow, "has the power to make you pay attention and understand" (299).

Critique

Elbow's critics have faulted him for his individualistic understanding of power relations. Irwin Hashimoto, reviewing *Writing with Power,* suggests that Elbow's strategies neglect the importance of students' knowledge about the subject matter and conventions of the specific discipline within which they are writing (Murray and Hashimoto 211). In his 1971 piece "The Way Out," Bruffee accused Elbow of encouraging the "rampant individualism" (463) that Elbow said he abhorred in his students by neglecting to structure an alternative, collective version of authority in the classroom. Greg Myers and James Berlin confronted the issue of power in a larger context. Myers concluded that Elbow's approach precludes "any analysis of the social conditions of our writing" ("Reality" 165). Berlin agreed, noting that in Elbow's work "political change can only be considered by individuals and in individual terms" ("Rhetoric and Ideology" 486). And while Susan Jarratt has suggested that Elbow's "believing game" could stifle less powerful voices in particular contexts (109–10), Thomas O'Donnell sees Elbow's practice as encouraging students to listen to those voices (Babin and Harrison 130). I agree with O'Donnell, and I believe that the capacity to listen and temporarily inhabit the perspectives of another with the depth and intellectual honesty that Elbow's extended practice invites could be the most important thing we can teach, and learn, in the current political and human strife of 2016.[26]

Peter Elbow's work is an enormous contribution to the literature on the teaching of writing. His conceptually sophisticated insights into the complexity of writing anxiety and his intelligently wrought solutions have empowered many of us, both individually and in groups, to take action with our writing that we might not otherwise have dared to. Much like Rogerian psychology, with which it shares similarities, Elbow's work has given many writers faith in themselves. And he has helped broaden the means of persuasion in the field by teaching and writing nonadversarial argument—arguing *for* a stance, rather than *against* an opposing stance. He does this consistently from invention techniques, to peer interaction, to reading techniques, to interacting with colleagues, to modeling this method in his own writing.

After my early critiques of Elbow in papers I gave at CCCC as a graduate student, both Sherrie Gradin and John Trimbur separately asked me to reconsider. Trimbur suggested I look at my own writing process to discover whether I used Elbow's practices. In fact, the only way I finished my dissertation was to start freewriting and begin compartmentalizing "believing" and "doubting" my own words. Indulging in an uncontrolled fantasy of imaginary "doubting" responses from possible readers of my work can freeze me in fear even as I write these words. Thanks to Elbow's role in the Brooklyn Institute, my own collaborative practices are balanced in a reciprocal interaction between the individual and the group—however their definitions are constantly revised.[27]

Dewey believed that this kind of fluid interaction is crucial to a functioning US democracy, and should take place in an environment with exposure to various perspectives and attention to material conditions. Has our current cultural insularity, caused in part by gerrymandered political districts and ideologically homogeneous cable news channels, degraded an environment ideally conducive to democracy? In the wake of the unjust killings in July 2016 of Alton Sterling in Baton Rouge and of Philando Castile in St. Paul, and the subsequent killings of police officers Lorne Ahrens, Michael Krol, Michael J. Smith, Brent Thompson, and Patrick Zamarripa in Dallas, Barack Obama asked US citizens to temporarily inhabit

the perspectives of both Black Lives Matter protesters and police officers in order to begin a process that could lead away from violence
toward peaceful reform. We do not often feel the need to consider
ideas outside our comfort zones. But Dewey, Elbow, and Obama
form an unlikely alliance in asking us to save our democracy by
listening carefully before we act.

KENNETH A. BRUFFEE: THE FACE
OF COLLABORATIVE LEARNING

> I'm happy to admit how much I agree with your piece, and how
> much I learn from it—particularly regarding the question of how
> to promote or advocate collaboration without simply trying to
> force it. It's just that, because you cast me in the adversary role,
> you make me feel as though I have to recant to say this when I
> don't feel I'm recanting at all but rather benefitting from an ally.
> —Peter Elbow, "Comment on Ken Bruffee,"
> *College English* (December 1972)

Bruffee's 1972 article "The Way Out" marked his entry into the
public fray over innovative teaching methods. He included Elbow
among those whose antiauthoritarian pedagogy promotes individualism rather than collective authority. Elbow's public response
to Bruffee's attack in the December 1972 issue of *College English*
began what was to become a fruitful (and good-natured) ideological rivalry between the two advocates of group practice. Although
Bruffee's "Way Out" was for the most part a reaction to antiestablishment pedagogy, he concluded with a brief description of what
he termed *collaborative learning,* a kind of student group work
which if carefully thought out, he said, could change the structure
of power in the classroom. A year later *College English* published his
"Collaborative Learning: Some Practical Models."

Bruffee was a writing program administrator at Brooklyn College during CUNY's shift from selective admissions to open admissions in 1970. He would later say that his frequent breakfast
discussions with other CUNY administrators (including Mina

Shaughnessy, Harvey Weiner, and Donald McQuade) contributed significantly to his understanding of knowledge as a social, conversational phenomenon. His colleague Richard Sterling tells the story of this group in "Bruffee and the CUNY Circle." Among the books they read together were Dewey's *Experience and Education* and Paulo Freire's *Pedagogy of the Oppressed*. One of the ideas that came out of these breakfasts was peer tutoring, and it was in the training of peer tutors that Bruffee was to elaborate his version of collaborative pedagogy. "The Brooklyn Plan: Attaining Intellectual Growth through Peer-Group Tutoring" is Bruffee's description of that process.[28] Bruffee found, first, that peers made better tutors than graduate students or teachers because they could overcome the underprepared students' emotional resistance to an alien academic culture. Second, Bruffee discovered that the best way to train peer tutors was to give them a writing course built around a series of essay-like peer critiques, in which they critiqued one another's work. Third, and most consequentially, Bruffee found that these peer tutors became better, more confident, and more intellectually secure writers themselves.[29] This third effect of the peer-tutor training process helped move Bruffee's interest into the theoretical and philosophical underpinnings and implications of collaborative learning.

Bruffee's social-constructionist theory draws on the work of Thomas Kuhn, Richard Rorty, Stanley Fish, and Lev Vygotsky, and it is consistent with the US pragmatism of George Herbert Mead and John Dewey. Knowledge is socially conceived and negotiated, in this view, authority is based in community agreement, and social relations are based on reciprocal interaction. Citing early social-constructionist moves in the profession, Bruffee defines collaborative learning "sometimes as a process that constitutes fields or disciplines of study and sometimes as a pedagogical tool that 'works' in teaching composition and literature" ("Collaborative Learning and the 'Conversation of Mankind'" 635). In relation to the teaching of writing, Bruffee takes the emphasis off peer editing and replaces it with peer conversation. "What students do when working collaboratively on their writing," Bruffee says, is not write or edit or, least of all, read proof. What they do is converse. They talk about the subject and about the assignment. They talk through the writer's understanding of the subject. They converse about their own relationship and, in general, about relationships in an academic or intellectual context between students and teachers. Most of all they converse about and as a part of writing. (645)

There is a consistent relationship between Bruffee's collaborative practice and his social-constructionist theory.

Bruffee's *Short Course in Writing*, published first in 1972, has served as the primary college textbook for teaching writing using collaborative learning.[30] Bruffee's approach to peer criticism is a modification of the peer-review process of professional journals; it is dialogic in structure. His approach, which emphasizes the process of negotiation, complements Elbow's focus on invention. Bruffee's ideal class for the peer-critique sequence is a semester-long course in which students have time to practice the steps of the peer critique cumulatively.

Although Bruffee's collaborative learning calls for much verbal discussion about academic and literary topics among students in small groups, as I described in the previous chapter, his peer criticism, which I will focus on for the purposes of this chapter, involves a series of exercises in which students "converse" in written responses to one another. The students are assigned five short papers and ten peer responses over the course of a semester. For Paper 1, the teacher assigns a persuasive essay of three to four paragraphs on a topic of the student's choice (53–84). When the first paper is due, the class sits in a circle and students read their papers aloud, one at a time, no response. Instead of handing the papers in to the teacher, however, students trade papers with one another and begin the first stage of the process of peer criticism, the descriptive stage. The descriptive stage is followed, in the response to the next paper, by the evaluative stage, and, to the paper after that, by the substantive stage. By the fourth paper, all stages of peer response are in play. Students have traded with one another and with "mediator" peers who resolve differences of opinion. They have responded to one another at each step of the process. The fifth and final paper completes the series with a final author's response, which, as well as giving the author a say on what everybody has said about his or her papers up until then, also gives the author a chance to discuss the semester-long process he or she has just experienced.[31]

For Bruffee the advantage of such an approach is that it underscores the interactional and conversational nature of the learning process while students learn descriptive, evaluative, and substantive analytical skills ("Brooklyn Plan" 450). Bruffee's intent is twofold: on the one hand he believes collaborative learning is the best way for teachers (representatives of various academic and professional communities) to induct students into the communities they have ostensibly opted to join. On the other hand, Bruffee believes that collaborative learning represents a clear affirmation on a practical scale of the thoroughly social nature of human discourse. Bruffee draws on Rorty for his definition of knowledge as "socially justified belief." For Bruffee all three words are significant—*social, justification,* and *belief.* Bruffee takes from Rorty the notion that "to learn something is to cause 'a shift in a person's relations with others, not a shift inside the person which now *suits* him to enter such new relationships'" ("Liberal Education" 105). Justifying, according to Bruffee, involves the process in which belief becomes knowledge. "To justify a belief is to establish a certain kind of relationship among ourselves and among the things we say" (105). Beliefs, according to Bruffee, are "private and particular to ourselves," and in some sense derived from "contact with the world through our senses" (104). To socially justify our beliefs, then, means to establish relationships—among words and among people. Bruffee's collaborative practice is consistent with this definition of knowledge in that it is built upon a structure of relationships among words and paragraphs and among people.

Teaching, according to Bruffee, involves introducing students "both to the beliefs currently assented to by the community of liberally educated people and to the ways judgments are made, socially justified, and assented to by that community" ("Liberal Education" 108). The purpose is to develop critical thinking as a social activity.

Bruffee wants students to understand the participatory nature of knowledge so that they can learn to question it effectively (109). Bruffee's assumptions about authority in the classroom are directly related to his assumptions about knowledge. "Our authority as teachers always derives directly or indirectly from the prevailing conception of the authority of knowledge" ("Collaborative Learning and the 'Conversation of Mankind'" 649). Concepts of knowledge are historically based (Bruffee draws on Rorty's historicist analysis of Cartesian and post-Cartesian philosophy to make this point), and changing conceptions of knowledge require changing other assumptions and practices of our disciplines, including most significantly the role of the teacher. For Bruffee, a concept of knowledge as grounded in social participation implies a restructuring of authority in the classroom. In "Collaborative Learning: Some Practical Models" Bruffee maintains that the teacher must reinterpret, not abdicate, the role:

> The teacher must reconceive his role. He must become an organizer of people into communities for a specific purpose—learning. He must reapportion freedom and discipline within the class, thereby establishing a "poly-centralized" collaborative learning community in which the teacher moves to the perimeter of the action, once the scene is set. The central action then is people learning. It is important to see that the teacher does not simply take a laissez-faire attitude, abrogating his responsibility to educate. He reinterprets this responsibility. The teacher understands that his primary job is to organize the learning community, because, as Dewey points out, "community life does not organize itself in an enduring way purely spontaneously. It requires thought and planning ahead." (637)

The teacher's job in Bruffee's pedagogy, then, is not to become a member of the group as is the case in Elbow's pedagogy, but to act as architect of the intellectual and social relationships in the classroom. Having done this, the teacher's job is to step back, enforcing the rules when necessary and fulfilling his or her institutional obligation to grade papers. Many advocates of innovative pedagogy have noted that students can have a difficult time adjusting to a new interpretation of authority in the classroom. Bruffee maintains this position as well, but he goes further, claiming that the teacher may also resist a restructuring of his or her role: "[T]he teacher will have to be wary of his own tendency . . . to lapse back into the traditional patterns of dominance and passivity" (642). This is also a problem that students face in their roles as peer critics, Bruffee says, noting the danger that students will tend to take on the role of "little teachers," subverting the strengths of the peer relationship, which is ideally reciprocal ("Brooklyn Plan" 463). In Bruffee's peer criticism, the critique carries as much status as the paper it responds to, and it carries with it the responsibility that that status accrues. Any point a critic makes she has to defend in a well-supported and coherent paragraph. This gives the author either a good reason to change something in his paper or an argument against which he can defend himself. The critical thinking required of both author and critic in Bruffee's version of collaborative learning restructures authority in a subtle but significant way. The critic's responsibility for presenting a full-bodied and coherent critique provides the author with more information for consequently "taking the role of the other" in thinking through appropriate action. Dewey's insistence on interaction and continuity is reflected in Bruffee's attention to structuring group work and his cumulative series of peer critiques. In his commitment to structure and guidance from the teacher, Bruffee is following in Dewey's footsteps.

Critique

Bruffee's work has been controversial from the start, as evidenced by the activity in the "Comment and Response" section of *College English* in issues following the publication of his major articles. His critics hail from the right and from the left. Early critics from the right, such as Thomas Johnson (76) and Pedro Beade (708) accused Bruffee of totalitarianism. Bruffee's defense to the critique from the right has been to explain the importance of diversity in collaborative learning and the necessary reciprocal and constantly shifting interplay between the individual and the group. Bruffee contends that conformity results from the imposition of ideas in a hierarchical structure (e.g., Hitler's) rather than the horizontally structured social negotiation of ideas that characterizes his type of collaborative learning. A second response: to say that knowledge is consensual and emerges from social negotiation is not to deny the importance of individuals. Pragmatist thought, which Bruffee is clearly representing in his work, recognizes the importance of individuals in society, since the idiosyncratic perspective of the individual provides the basis of new ideas and social reconstruction. Whether Bruffee motivates that voice acceptably is another matter, and this is related to whether or not his ideal of consensus with conflict actually works in practice.

Leftist critics such as Greg Myers and James Sledd argue that Bruffee's collaborative learning is problematic because, in Sledd's words, it ignores "the world outside the universities" (585). While agreeing that Bruffee's methods do a good job of teaching students to write ("Greg Myers Responds" 213), Myers also accuses Bruffee of ignoring the larger social context of writing by concentrating on what his students have in common (an ostensible desire to join a community of knowledgeable peers), rather than the socioeconomic differences that separate them. In ignoring his students' social differences, Myers says, Bruffee is by implication perpetuating "the provision of different kinds of knowledge for the rich and the poor" ("Reality, Consensus, and Reform" 167). Trimbur's "critique from within" questions whether seeking consensus is enough of a pull to bring out differences and promote the conflict necessary for a true consensus building. Trimbur's focus is not on difference itself, as is Elbow's, but on the engagement of differences within collaborative-learning groups and the motivation necessary to make that happen. This area represents an Elbow-Bruffee distinction. Elbow's concern is with bringing out maximum differences within a group; Bruffee *assumes* maximum differences within a group and sets up conditions for them to be engaged. Trimbur believes that differences should be engaged, but proposes dissensus as a goal in some group work in order to ensure multiple ideas and encourage creativity.

I agree with Trimbur, and I have found his dissensus exercises to be useful in classes I've taught. However, I contend that consensus has been a bugbear that has been misunderstood and thus masks both the value of Bruffee's work and possibly more insightful critiques of it—much like the controversies around Elbow's work. Myers from the left and Beade from the right accuse Bruffee of promoting conformity in his use of the technique of consensus. I would agree with them if consensus were used rigidly in Bruffee's pedagogy, but in fact it is rarely achieved. Even in the small groups, Bruffee insists on the privilege of a "dissenting vote." Dissensus, in fact, was a significant part of the experience of the Brooklyn Institute fellows in the summer of 1980, and it productively affected how we managed dissensus in our classes thereafter (see Holt, "Importance of Dissent").

Consensus as a heuristic can be valuable as a method to motivate students to argue the issues at hand, rather than come up with "individual" answers and complacently turn to discussing their weekend experiences. In describing an early experiment in collaborative learning conducted by M. L. J. Abercrombie (described in her *Anatomy of Judgment*), Bruffee describes what happened when a group of medical students began to make diagnoses collaboratively, rather than individually.

> Through the process of struggling toward a consensus in order to resolve a diagnostic problem, the students first uncovered the biases and limitations others brought to the judgmental task, only to discover, second and most importantly, the biases and limitations which they brought to it themselves. ("Brooklyn Plan" 454)

In short, consensus is used as a tool to bring out differences, to open up discussion, and to complicate issues.

In Bruffee's collaborative learning, the teacher designs practical classroom experience for collective empowerment. In consciously developing a collaborative pedagogical theory based on social-constructionist thought, Bruffee developed the most fully collaborative composition pedagogy that recognizes and incorporates the formative quality of social interaction. He adapted the social implications of an egalitarian, pragmatist notion of knowledge to classroom practices that effectively enable students to invest collaboration with authority. As I interpret his work, Bruffee hopes that change in the larger political structure can be accomplished partly by enabling students to acquire the tools of social participation. But he does stop short of seeing the collaborative classroom as a tool for political change. His site of reformation is the academy.[32]

Elbow's and Bruffee's pedagogies help structure classrooms to encourage diversity in our students. If the students are heterogeneous in the classroom, and everyone chooses to speak, diversity can make its case with the pedagogies of Bruffee and Elbow. If not, it can't. Given the mass-media domination of postmodern culture and the homogeneous nature of many of our student populations, we cannot count on a diversity of voices in the classroom to complicate students' notions of knowledge and subjectivities. Neither Bruffee's nor Elbow's texts focus specifically on culture and difference as a topic in the writing classroom.[33]

I have shown ways in which Elbow's and Bruffee's collaborative practices exemplify facets of pragmatism—Elbow's focus on the individual nevertheless enacts a remarkably agile ontology of play and freedom—a postmodern version of pragmatist sociologist Mead's dialectical subject. Bruffee's extrapolation of the dialectical subject into classroom social relations is well-structured and exhibits Dewey's minimal criteria of interaction and continuity with a strong role for the teacher as designer of classroom activity. Bruffee's focus on Rorty's pragmatism, however, distracts him from his early acknowledgment of the importance of material conditions to an understanding of collaborative learning. Neither Elbow's nor Bruffee's collaborative learning displays the thick historical description that is crucial to Dewey's reformist work. That significant pragmatist strength is represented by the later collaborative work of Ira Shor, to whom I will turn next.

IRA SHOR: THE "TRANSLATOR"
OF FREIRE'S CRITICAL PEDAGOGY

[H]ope, as an ontological need, demands an anchoring in practice. . . . That is why there is no hope in sheer hopefulness.

—Paulo Freire and Ana Maria Anaújo Freire,
Pedagogy of Hope (1994)

Critical pedagogy is a loose term associated with cultural studies,
contact zones, and radical pedagogies. The goal of critical pedagogy is cultural critique. Not all critical pedagogy is collaborative;
in fact, most of it is concerned more with political critique than
with classroom practice. Shor's 1996 book *When Students Have
Power* gave critical pedagogy a major voice on collaborative practice. Under the umbrella of Dewey's work, Shor draws on both
Bruffee's and Elbow's methods and contributes to the literature on
collaborative learning with his attention to negotiated curricula and
to the sociohistorical-political-economic situation of his students
and his teaching. Shor's contribution to collaborative learning lies
in his meticulous and ongoing investigation of the material circumstances of students. His careful observations lead to a series of
negotiations with students, rather than to collaborative templates.

In *When Students Have Power* Shor describes his collaborative
methods as they emerge in one course. Shor bases his work on a
foundation of Deweyan reflective practice extended by the social-
justice concerns of Freire, with whom Shor worked to develop a
critical pedagogy appropriate to American education. Throughout
the book, Shor refers to Dewey, who he says elsewhere "drew attention to the *class* bias built into the education system" (*Culture
Wars* 49). In *When Students Have Power,* Shor's careful construction
of teacher roles and student relations and his scrupulous account-
ing of material conditions reflect Dewey's influence. Freire's influence is demonstrable in Shor's process of beginning critical inquiry
with students' classroom chairs and fast food—what is directly in
their view. Freire's influence is also seen in Shor's privileging of the
teacher-student relationship, and in his use of utopian contrasts.

Shor observes in his students contradictions between their commitment to individualism and faith in themselves on the one hand and the demoralizing and frustrating circumstances of their daily lives on the other. "Hegemony usually works best," Shor says, "when it hides its own operation, and it does appear that my students generally feel freely in control of their 'real selves' while not freely in control of their time, bodies, or money, because of schooling, work, commuting, family, the cost of living, etc." (*When* 103). Using the heuristic of utopian contrasts, Shor asks his students to compare their current situations with ideal situations. By teaching a course on concepts of Utopia, Shor hopes to stimulate his students' imaginations about possibilities in their lives, while enabling conditions in which students begin to make possibility a reality in the classroom. Realizing that their material circumstances are a product of larger systemic issues can be debilitating to students' motivation without the simultaneous realization that they are not alone in seeking solutions. Collapsing the binary between students' faith in individualism and their fatalism about the circumstances of their daily lives can be productive only in the context of collaboration. Their faith in individual initiative must be expanded to include faith in the power of collective action to ensure that action, and not despair, is the result. This is why collaborative work is crucial to Shor's success.

Shor works from Dewey's definition of experience, which includes an examination of the material conditions of one's life. He describes his working-class students and their material circumstances down to their clothes and the condition of their teeth. He describes the windowless classroom, the traffic noise, and the nearly unbreathable air (38). His most impressive move is a detailed examination of the effect of parking problems on student attrition, concluding that "every pedagogy . . . is dependent on the larger social conditions enveloping every learning process" (181). One of Shor's goals is to decentralize the authority of the instructor in order to stymie the cynical games that jaded students engage in to get through college courses. He calls this state of alienation the "Siberian Syndrome," and he contextualizes this state of affairs in terms of authoritarian schooling and the conservative political culture of the 1980s.

Given the frustrating circumstances and lack of agency in his students' personal lives, Shor analyzes the "knowledge, relations, and power" in his classroom, particularly in the context of his students' experience. His research method is a rhetorical analysis of discourse relations: "Who is addressing whom in what setting, at what time, in what kind of language, for what reason and purpose, and with what result?" Shor asks (66). Bringing these questions into the classroom, Shor focuses on the students associated with the Siberian Syndrome who sit together at the back of the room, with body language that says "too cool for school." He notices that they habitually address one another, not him. When they do address him, they do so in a language of boredom and resistance for the purpose of simultaneously resisting and submitting to him. The result is that they don't learn anything.

The antidote to this systemic poison, according to Shor, is the teacher's sharing authority with students through a complex process of negotiating the course syllabus, grading standards, and class procedures. Shor's goal is for students to develop ability and the will to address one another and him assertively for the purpose of negotiating for control of their education. Shor hopes that they learn not only about the course topic but also how to act collectively in their own best interests. Shor eloquently describes his approach:

> By opening the process to student authority, power-sharing repositions students from being cultural exiles to becoming cultural constituents, from being unconsulted curriculum-receivers to becoming collaborative curriculum-makers. In this way, a negotiated syllabus challenges the Siberian Syndrome, creating the option for students to be leaders and stakeholders in the process. (200)

Shor's pedagogy is not only collaborative in involving students in co-constructing the curriculum; he also employs an array of fairly standard collaborative learning activities. These include project groups, peer-revision groups, and small-group discussions of course readings. Students talk over his proposals for the course syllabus and grading procedures before discussing them as a whole class, and they engage in small-group evaluations of one another's project-group presentations. He also formed voluntary "after-class groups" that discuss that day's class, extending the discussion but also critiquing it, including Shor's role. Suggestions made by the after-class groups are then discussed and voted on by the whole class at the next meeting.

Shor gives students opportunities to develop their own discourse and ideas about a topic prior to any input from the instructor. He calls this "frontloading." As teacher, he waits until student groups have spoken and some class discussion has occurred before weighing in with any of his own comments. This is "backloading." Shor describes the process:

> After they wrote for some minutes, the students reported their ideas so I could list them on the board. I then asked them to reflect on the items so as to classify themes, after which five items emerged as their self-perceived categories. . . . I then asked students to divide themselves voluntarily into groups, one for each theme. The groups met in class, did free writing for ten minutes on their chosen theme, read their texts, held discussion, and then reported serially to the class, with each group posing a question to begin the larger dialogue. As groups reported and posed questions, I re-presented their material to the class, took notes, and posed my own backloaded questions and comments. (155)

Note that Shor is careful not to intervene in or micromanage student work groups. This fact and his use of frontloading student discourse is central to how he uses collaborative learning to overcome the Siberian Syndrome, to engage students as active stakeholders in the discourse of the class.

On the importance of relinquishing professorial frontloading, he comments that he wanted "to take advantage of a democratizing structure in collaborative learning, that is, its creation of students-only groups that exclude teacher-talk and thus can develop student discourse relatively distant from the teacher's idiom and values" (48). This is important early in a course, Shor notes, to establish the value of student discourse and to create a safe atmosphere for participation (48). Shor's practice of taking copious notes of the group reports and at times quoting back to students from them also reinforces the message that he values what they have to say.[34]

For Shor, the heart of teaching is a fluid and negotiable relationship between student and teacher. Shor's term *cogovernance* exemplifies the complexity he attempts to embody: "A cogoverning teacher has special responsibilities to launch and maintain the process but not sole authority in it or over it" (122–23). A strong teacher role is evident in the after-class groups. Believing that teacher frontloading can set up passive resistance, Shor focuses his behavior on what he can learn from the students (a form of empiricism, or experience). Backloading teacher comments, speaking after the students have spoken, is a technique that gives Shor a chance to use what he has learned from listening to students to determine what he will say next. By the end of the book Shor has redefined the teacher role with the interesting term *teacher sites*. A teacher site can be occupied by anyone, provisionally (200). In a Foucauldian moment, Shor says, "Authority is a moving target from term to term and even week to week within a term" (90).

Shor's commitment to collaborative ideology is evident not only in his management of classroom discourse, but also in the discourse he writes. Refusing the academic convention of agonistic discourse, Shor generously cites Dewey, Bruffee, and feminist Nancy Schniedewind (47), among others, revealing his connection to them, rather than his distinction from them. Shor enacts what feminist Catherine Fox suggests by maintaining an attitude of self-interrogation throughout the book, for instance, "Of course, I ask myself right now if I am merely searching for excuses to explain away my discomfort with not always meeting student expectations" (150). In displaying his second thoughts, he shows us how he works against his desire for control as a teacher: "Being in control may help my self-image and my professional image, but the truth is that it guarantees nothing about student learning" (106). In discussing Shor's struggle with control, John Borczon notes the inconsistencies between what Shor says and how he says it: the focus on his students in the classroom morphs into a focus on himself in the book (72).

Critique

Questions remain about the application of Shor's methods to middle-class students. Marge Murray's experience with students at the University of Pennsylvania, for example, is described in her article "A Radical Pedagogy of Composition." Murray's political goals in the classroom were so much at odds with the values of her students that she felt ineffective at both tasks—preparing students to write for academic and professional communities and promoting political consciousness. Although the distinction in political agendas between students and teachers is a problem in all pedagogies, the radical teacher attempting collaborative pedagogy with a Marxist approach is faced with a high risk of disaffection in most middle-class student populations. Trimbur, who has taught at affluent Worcester Polytechnic Institute (and is now at Emerson College) embraces another perspective. Trimbur contends that some critical pedagogy essentializes middle-class students as uninterested in the politics of reform. The middle class from a Marxist perspective, he says, is neither stable nor homogeneous; rather it is subject to an unstable tug-of-war between labor and capital, as Barbara Ehrenreich demonstrates in *Fear of Falling*. If brought into the discourse of layoffs and the shrinking of the middle class due to corporate domination of labor, Trimbur argues, students may find some familiar ground in their own family histories and those of their friends ("Politics" 201). Trimbur has nothing but praise for Shor's attention to the material conditions of pedagogy. Min-Zhan Lu and Bruce Horner single Shor out as a positive example as well, noting a version of his self-critical stance—that he departs from the too-common practice of labeling students' perspectives false consciousness and teachers' perspectives the one true way. They note that Shor could improve by inviting students into the analysis of material conditions not only for themselves, but also for teachers, possibly changing their high, unilateral, consumerist expectations of teachers (274–75).

Shor pays close attention to Dewey's criteria of interaction and continuity in each step of his pedagogy. An example is the after-class group, in which Shor's students give immediate feedback about what went on in class and negotiate for what they want to happen in the next class. They also decide what they want to bring to a vote in the next class, thus extending the feedback session to the larger group. In addition to meeting Dewey's criteria of interaction and continuity, Shor's immersion in the discourse of material conditions is close to the spirit of Dewey's Laboratory School. As Trimbur suggests in reference to *Education Limited,* a book on critical pedagogy from the Education Group II of the University of Birmingham Department of Cultural Studies, "radical educators need to develop a critical vocationalism that sees students not so much as postmodern subjects defined by the semiosis of a postindustrial media and consumer society but as producers of the material conditions of life" (Trimbur, "Politics" 205). Shor stands as an exemplar in US critical pedagogy of one who takes classroom practice seriously and uses sophisticated and contingent collaborative practices to set up conditions for his students to enact critical thinking about their economic circumstances in the context of the culture. What Shor doesn't focus on—replicating much Marxist practice—is cultural, race, and gender inequity. Nina Chordas has noted that Shor uses the word *equality* as if it is not problematic in terms of cultural and other differences (218).

RACE AND RACISM

One of the significant gaps in the field is scholarship on collaborative practice specifically focused on race and racism. As Catherine Prendergast, Jennifer Clary-Lemon, and Victor Villanueva have suggested, racism has been largely missing from our disciplinary discussions, even as our field has benefited from the Open Admissions protests that spurred its development in the early 1970s in New York (Franco). And because a collection of materials on implementation of the *Students' Right to Their Own Language* (SR-TOL) was initiated but never realized, teachers and scholars have lost insight into what might have been the most valuable impact of

SRTOL on pedagogy (Smitherman 365 and Parks 206–10). Valuable early contributions were Stokely Carmichael's Freedom School (see Schneider) and Citizenship Schools in the South (see Kates and Lathan). In "Working with Difference: Critical Race Theory and the Teaching of Composition," Gary Olson provides an overview of the area as it relates to students' identity and the teaching of writing. His chapter is an excellent rebuttal to the idea of "racelessness" in the composition classroom; he contends that critical race theory can help teachers see the value in recognizing race as a factor and thus confront it head-on when appropriate, rather than pretend that racism no longer exists (218). Most of what is available on collaborative learning as it relates to race, however, comes from antiracist pedagogy as it is practiced in education departments.

Antiracist pedagogy is embraced by an affiliation of scholars who emphasize the structural aspects of racism and the effects of that endemic racism on people of color. The movement commonly called "critical race theory" started in the 1970s with a group of lawyers who were interested in interrogating and reforming the subtle discriminations of the law, and though it still most accurately describes this activist movement in the field of law, by the twenty-first century scholars and activists in many fields were using the umbrella of critical race theory to describe their work. Some of the research by educators has shown that collaborative work and a community approach to education is helpful in responding to the effects of racism on students of color.

Laurence Parker and David O. Stovall note that antiracist pedagogy differs from critical pedagogy in its emphasis. Whereas critical pedagogy focuses on the structural inequities in schools and the impact of the media on racism and classism in the culture, it often takes a multicultural approach, which neglects the particular circumstances of different groups of people of color and how they experience racism. Antiracist pedagogy is in some sense a complement to critical pedagogy, one that focuses on the experiences of African Americans or Latinx, starting with giving students a foundation of the history of racism and moving to storytelling by people of color. Why is the storytelling important, and how does it differ or reflect expressive rhetorics in the field of composition? To answer that question, I will point out what Parker and Stovall see as the assumptions behind their pedagogy.

To explain why it is important that antiracist research and pedagogy exist to complement critical pedagogy, Parker and Stovall cite three assumptions. First, the experiences of people of color are crucial to this kind of work because of their history, culture, and day-to-day confrontations with racism. Second, this experience can be informative about human interaction, and, third, teachers must develop practices "that help generate knowledge designed to describe, analyze and empower people of color and to help change negative social forces into positive social forces as they impact on everyday life." For this to happen, according to Parker and Stovall, teachers, scholars, and administrators should "know not only the history of race and race relations, but also the connection of race to a community of interest with regard to the group's struggle for power and self-determination" (174). Storytelling puts students of color in the role of informant to the teacher-researcher, giving the teacher valuable information to help him or her design research, and eventually pedagogy, to face up to racist assumptions, rather than unconsciously validate them. Storytelling is a way for students to instruct teachers on the forms and effects of racism so they can design pedagogy to combat it.

Along with storytelling, antiracist pedagogy focuses on community above competition, and collaborative learning is a pedagogy that fits with this purpose. Toward that end, Parker and Stovall advocate "culture-centric" schools. Students, teachers, and community members in culture-centric schools work together in a broad collaboration to research African American culture, history, and traditions. This work provides a framework, a validation, and a nurturing experience for students. Parker and Stovall look to these schools as models for education reform.

Marvin Lynn offers a justification and critique of critical race pedagogy in his article "Inserting the 'Race' into Critical Pedagogy: An Analysis of 'Race-Based Epistemologies,'" published in *Educational Philosophy and Theory*. Noting that the movement began with lawyers, Lynn defines critical race pedagogy as "an analysis of racial, ethnic and gender subordination in education that relies mostly upon the perceptions, experiences and counter-hegemonic practices of educators of color" (154). Anticipating possible accusations of essentialism, he explains that this pedagogy is not essentialist, but realist (161). "Objective" or "neutral" legal theory and pedagogy do not take into account the reality of racism, but subjective experience does (156). A critique could be made, he says, that the pedagogical practice of storytelling often relies on subjective narration without attention to the history of race relations and culture that is the source of the narrators' experiences. He recommends that critical race pedagogy include

1. teaching children about the importance of African culture;
2. dialogical engagement in the classroom;
3. engaging in daily acts of self-affirmation; and
4. resisting and challenging hegemonic administrators. (154)

Lynn's overall argument is that taking advantage of the commonalities between critical race theory and Afrocentric education can help create a critical race pedagogy (162).

Community is a common thread in the collaborative practice that I have analyzed in this chapter. Elbow and Belanoff's *Community of Writers* is designed for the anxious student writer. Bruffee's "community of knowledgeable peers" constructs knowledge. Shor's students form a community to survive and transcend the economic conditions that thwart them. For critical race theorists, community can provide a place safe from racism and serve as a strategy for students to educate teachers about the racism they experience. In the next chapter I will discuss community as it pertains to feminist pedagogy.

5

Feminist Pedagogy

> The Marxist and Freireian roots of Berlin's social-epistemic brand of rhetoric and writing instruction are those of feminist pedagogy, too.
>
> —Susan Hunter, "A Woman's Place *Is* in the Composition Classroom" (1991)

THE LATE-TWENTIETH-CENTURY WOMEN'S MOVEMENT with its consciousness-raising groups came partly out of the Civil Rights Movement and the Vietnam War protests, when many women discovered that their interests had been left out of the political agenda. Although women who had worked alongside men in the Civil Rights Movement were equally neglected, most did not join white women to protest patriarchy because racism was a more significant oppression, one largely ignored by the predominantly white feminist movement until the late 1980s, when the protests of women of color led to US feminism's third wave. Feminism itself has mutated and evolved through several "waves," various material conditions, and new technology. The early focus on decentering teacher authority and resisting patriarchy has broadened to an acceptance of fluid identities, resistance to multiple sites of power, and politically strategic affiliations.

In the first part of this chapter I analyze the canonical work of second-wave feminists Nancy Schniedewind and Carolyn Shrewsbury, who defined feminist pedagogy for 1980s and 1990s feminist teachers as a clearly structured model in line with Kenneth Bruffee's and John Dewey's preferences. In the second part of the chapter I turn to the pivotal work published by Amie A. Macdonald and Susan Sánchez-Casal in their edited collection *Twenty-First-Century*

Feminist Classrooms: Pedagogies of Identity and Difference. Drawing on both pragmatism and transnational feminism, Macdonald and Sánchez-Casal promote feminist pedagogy as moving beyond identity theory to a fluid intersectionality in which students are encouraged to make provisional alliances with other students to reach specific political goals. Characteristic of the twentieth and twenty-first-century pedagogies I address is a belief that established knowledge is a tool used by the hegemonic mainstream to subjugate the marginalized subject, that collective power is crucial to right the balance, and that authority should be destabilized in service of social justice. I argue that the feminist pedagogies I describe in this chapter represent a particularly effective use of collaborative pedagogy in that together they embody both the strengths of Dewey's pragmatism as social reform and the strengths of transnational feminism as a way to embrace fluid identities without giving up collective action.

Authority is the central theme in feminist pedagogies, with the desire to decenter or restructure it a crucial part of each version. Feminist pedagogy consistently strives to distribute authority, rather than give women control of it.[35] This stance works congruently with feminist notions of epistemology that understand knowledge to be multiperspectival. Although these pedagogies have a clear political agenda—to right the wrong that structures power inequitably in the academy and in society—the method is not political indoctrination, but rather an attempt to offer students skills to voice multiple perspectives that give students the power of choice. The method is tied to a philosophy of knowledge as socially constructed, with the hopeful agenda of further democratizing its construction. Scholars of feminist pedagogy restructure power, knowledge, and social relations in various ways.

How does resistance to authority play out in discussions of feminist teacher authority? An interdisciplinary review of the literature in 2002 by Lynne Webb, Myria Allen, and Kandi Walker reveals that teacher authority is given particular attention: we are cautioned that teachers' authority must be acknowledged, along with its limits and abuses. Webb, Allen, and Walker see in feminist pedagogy a softening of the teacher's role and an atmosphere that invites students' multiple voices to distribute authority in the classroom. When a feminist teacher complicates her authority in the classroom, she is representing knowledge as socially constructed, inviting multiple perspectives. Grace Scering's critical perspective is that schooling dominated by standardized testing has "neutralized" male dominance as "objectivity" (64). Thus, "connected knowing"—knowing connected to lived experience as opposed to "external knowing"—has been erased from the school system. "Redefinition of teacher authority as the activation of multiple perspectives leads to knowledge produced in conjunction with the social relations and strategies of a critical/feminist pedagogy," says Scering (66).

Scering notes the necessity for students to be taught democratic practices and the ability to, in Jesse Goodman's words, *"visualize democratic values within a broader societal and global context"* (64). In this context diversity is perceived as "lived differences [that surface] when community values rather than individualism receive attention" (66). Conceived this way, diversity is defined provisionally according to conflicts that emerge when people negotiate toward a common goal. Webb, Allen, and Walker see that a strong individual voice is important to this negotiation. Women are being taught, they suggest, what Sonja Foss and Cindy Griffin call "invitational rhetoric," or nonadversarial argument that leads to negotiative, rather than agonistic, discourse. Webb, Allen, and Walker end with suggestions about how to activate and disseminate feminist pedagogy within and beyond feminist circles. These include circulating their essay, using feminist pedagogy more deliberately, talking about the value of feminist pedagogy to colleagues, and converting men to the practice using the vocabulary of egalitarianism: "[I]n an educational environment in which change is constant and the student body is increasingly diverse, feminist pedagogy offers an inclusive teaching methodology for the twenty-first century" (71).

Susan Hunter suggests that in composition studies Webb, Allen, and Walker's goal has been reached. With the English Coalition Conference as evidence, Hunter sees feminist composition pedagogies as having merged with composition's emphasis on "critical inquiry, collaboration, and reflection; freewriting, dialectical notebooks, journals, writing to learn, peer reviews, small group discussions, portfolios, workshops, [and] conferences about drafts and revisions" (231–32). Arguing that "The Marxist and Freireian roots of Berlin's social-epistemic brand of rhetoric and writing instruction are those of feminist pedagogy, too" (232), Hunter views the merger as part of the wave of social construction.

SCHNIEDEWIND AND SHREWSBURY

Second-wave feminists Nancy Schniedewind's and Carolyn Shrewsbury's articles in *Women's Studies Quarterly* in 1987 are the canonical texts on feminist pedagogy that detail collaborative practices specifically for a women's-studies curriculum. Together Schniedewind and Shrewsbury outline a set of practices that fulfill Dewey's criteria of interaction and continuity, moving from classroom practice throughout the four years of the curriculum into the goal of reform of workplace environments. The focus on gendered power forms the content of the women's-studies curriculum they describe, but the practices are similar to Bruffee's, with students occupying various roles in classroom governance and the teacher as designer and enforcer of the new social structure.

Webb, Allen, and Walker's definition of feminist pedagogy— gleaned from their review of the literature—is taken from Carolyn Shrewsbury's article "What Is Feminist Pedagogy?" originally published in *Women's Studies Quarterly*. Shrewsbury defines feminist pedagogy as "a theory about the teaching/learning process that guides our choice of classroom practices by providing criteria to evaluate specific educational strategies and techniques in terms of the desired course goals or outcomes" (6). Shrewsbury's article and Schniedewind's "Teaching Feminist Process" stand as canonical works of feminist pedagogy for their clear articulation of feminist praxis, or theorypractice. Together the articles contribute a cogently argued and structured use of feminist pedagogy. Shrewsbury's article is a synthesis of themes of feminist pedagogy and an argument for its importance, while Schniedewind's is a guide to specific classroom and curricular practice designed to teach women students strategies to redistribute power first in the classroom and later in the workplace. Their goal is ambitious, much like Dewey's: to reform a patriarchal system using education as a method. Since their audience is women's-studies classes, the course content is feminism, not writing, but the process is similar to the best collaborative practices in writing classes.

Like Bruffee and Dewey, Schniedewind is cognizant of students' needs to learn how to redistribute power. As does Dewey in *Experience and Education,* Schniedewind says it's a mistake for instructors to attempt to "equalize power" in a classroom and expect students to automatically take responsibility (15). The teacher uses her expertise in what Schniedewind calls "feminist process" to teach students the roles they must take in order for that to happen (15–16). Echoing Dewey's criteria of interaction and continuity, feminist process in the classroom is not an end in itself, in Schniedewind's agenda. You teach feminist process so students can take it elsewhere (16). The student's personal experience is valued as it is contextualized in a community of others (classroom practices) and in its political, historical situation (readings). Valuing nonadversarial argument over agonistic rhetoric, students learn to respect differences among them and move through a methodological process to reach consensus, defined as a creative process in which the whole is more than the sum of its parts (24). Wholeness and integration are valued over fragmentation and dissonance possibly because of the agenda of unified political action. However, this focus creates an interesting tension, particularly given cultural and racial differences within groups. Even egalitarianism and democratic procedure are part of an ideology, not a neutral set of values.

Schniedewind includes in her list of feminist processes "(1) communicating, (2) developing a democratic group process, (3) cooperating, (4) integrating theory and practice, and (5) creating change" (15). Some specifics:

Students need to learn the difference between thoughts and feelings. Feelings are subjective states that should be shared, because, as Audre Lorde has said, they are the seed of action. Feelings themselves are not arguable. Thoughts, on the other hand, are subject to debate. As does Peter Elbow, Schniedewind recommends that students mark feeling statements with "I feel" (18). A technique for teaching students the difference between thoughts and feelings is to ask students to share first a feeling and then a thought. This exercise gives students an emotional vocabulary. As might happen in Bruffee's pedagogy with a similar task, the instructor keeps the time and keeps the students on task. They each have thirty seconds to respond, and they are allowed to pass.

Students need to learn how to give feedback. Sounding remarkably like Bruffee describing the first stage of his peer critique, Schniedewind says that feedback should be descriptive, not evaluative, specific, not general. Further, she says that feedback should focus on the behavior, not the person, and should consider the needs of both the receiver and the giver. To demonstrate these guidelines, she suggests that the teacher offer short hypothetical practice examples for students to respond to first poorly, then well, followed by class discussion (19).

Students need to practice shared leadership. Schniedewind defines shared leadership as "taking on the role that is needed in the group at the time" (20). Toward that end, the teacher can write a list of possible roles on the board, such as coordinator, focuser, includer, negotiator, timekeeper, and summarizer; ask students to reflect on what roles they've taken, on what roles they usually take; and set up situations in which they practice new roles, expanding their repertoires.

Although these specific skills, if practiced, can mitigate or preclude conflict, *a significant skill that students need to learn is conflict resolution.* Conflict resolution is important as a practice to move beyond dualism, beyond polarities, toward previously unimaginable creative solutions. One way this is accomplished is through a three-step procedure in which the two disagreeing parties first paraphrase each other's argument (to make sure they've got it right), then look for common ground, then together try to imagine one or more new perspectives on the situation. "The point is not for students to agree," says Schniedewind, "but to engage in dialogue rather than become locked into polar positions, and to generate new perspectives from which creative ideas or solutions may emerge." Another conflict-resolution skill is role reversal, which in this instance means "asking people involved in a conflict to take on the other's role" (21). A third is third-party mediation. It is important to note that Schniedewind surpasses Bruffee and Shor in her attention to conflict management. Both encourage healthy conflict, but there is no evidence that they teach students how to engage in it.

Schniedewind recommends that feminist process be taught at each level of the women's-studies curriculum. In the students' third year she recommends a fieldwork course in which students learn praxis, or the integration of theory and practice. She suggests participant observation in activist groups, for instance, to see how organizations put into practice their theory—or not. Finally in the senior year students should be given "skills for sustenance" in the form of networking and organizing. Students are taught how to form feminist networks in their post-college environments, to respond to sexist remarks, to do feminist workshops, and to be proactive feminists in whatever they do. She envisions teaching skills to students in their senior years that will help them make the transition to the workplace and set up feminist practice there. Schniedewind concludes by emphasizing the importance of sequencing these skills into the women's-studies curriculum and of offering them to faculty as well. Lack of these skills can deter organizational change. I am astonished by the good sense of this sequential curriculum. Students are habituated to feminist practice by graduation, in line with Dewey's goals of interaction and continuity and, ultimately, social reform.

Agency is emphasized in the relationship between theory, or beliefs, and practice, or acting on one's beliefs. This involves a kind of citizen's action leadership role, in which one is to use her agency by herself and in participation with others toward positive change. A person is always a potential change agent in any situation (20–21). Shrewsbury and Schniedewind see feminist pedagogy as actively utopian—involving participation among students, teachers, the community, and political actors—toward promoting constructive interactions among people to replace destructive conflict. The goal is to reform the university through "community, empowerment, and leadership" (Shrewsbury 8).

Twentieth-century US feminist pedagogy shares several themes with other versions of collaborative practice. These themes include interrogating authority, intersubjectifying epistemology, and offering strategies of democratic, political intervention through collaborative pedagogy. An offshoot of radical Marxist pedagogy, feminist pedagogy shares with Ira Shor's critical pedagogy a specific political agenda, with Bruffee's work a strict attention to classroom structure, and with Elbow's work an attention to the emotional aspects of learning. The contributions of each vein of collaborative learning—though sharing much in common—are distinctive and complementary in their strengths. They also share a major weakness—neglecting the complexities of difference. They assume the dominance of white, straight hegemony and then point at difference instead of recontextualizing the framework so that difference is not compartmentalized.

Ella Shohat, in her introduction to *Talking Visions: Multicultural Feminism in a Transnational Age* (2001), discusses how we are trained in this culture to think in terms of unity, of one voice, and not of hybridity. That there is uniformity reflected in feminist pedagogy as I have described it seems clear. The similarities are consistent across various descriptions of feminist pedagogy. Unresolved conflict is, reductively, bad; cooperation is good. The teacher is "decentered." Multiple perspectives replace objectivity. And yet, how multiple are the perspectives? They are remarkably consistent with those of a stereotypical middle-class, Anglo, Midwestern female subject—a polite subject who doesn't interrupt, who is "reasonable" in her actions, and who believes that differences are commensurable. Diversity is accounted for by the voices of multiple perspectives spoken in a group in which everyone listens in turn. Assuming that diverse voices will speak, multiple perspectives will be aired. With so much stress on resolving differences and reaching consensus, one wonders whether there is in certain circumstances a push toward the taming of difference.[36]

TWENTY-FIRST-CENTURY FEMINIST PEDAGOGIES

Some twenty-first-century feminist pedagogies attend to the differences among students without attenuating the authority of the group. The core issue is a power shift from the perception of a "group" or "community" as a stable, person-based entity to a notion of provisional alliance in which a subject is free to form alliances on the basis of issues, rather than personal identities. Rather than having to prioritize a single subject position (the rationale for strategic essentialism) a person is free to prioritize a particular subject position for a particular cause. Group power is dispersed, but at the same time increased because of the ability to stabilize temporarily for a particular task. For this to work, students must be aware of their various subject positions and the historical constructs that formed them. In this sense, twenty-first-century feminist pedagogy as I am describing it here recovers the strengths of Dewey's pragmatism in its reliance on historical situatedness. To explore the shift from "identity bonding" to "provisional alliance," I will first address the post-identity theory suggested by the work of Trinh T. Minh-ha to offer a more concrete description of how the shift might be reconceived in the individual; then I will describe the possible pedagogical reflections of that shift.

The careful negotiation of conflict in Schniedewind's pedagogy rests on the common assumption that difference produces conflict. It follows that one must resolve differences within or between groups before unity can be achieved, and that unity is a necessary condition for political action. Trinh questions that line of thought. In her frequently anthologized article "Not You/Like You: Postcolonial Women and the Interlocking Questions of Identity and Difference" (originally published in 1988), Trinh redefines difference as existing within the self, not just between selves. She recognizes the struggle between self and other as also a struggle *within* the self. The act of drawing boundaries between oneself and others requires that we focus on that which opposes us to others; we suppress that which connects us to others. "Identity, thus understood," says Trinh, "supposes that a clear dividing line can be made between I and not-I, . . . between us here and them over there" (929). The barriers we

have put up between ourselves, we have also put up within ourselves. They are in fact the same barriers. Trinh explains how we've
developed the sense of difference that opposes sameness—based on
segregation, separation, repression, and dominance—what she calls
"apartheid difference." We see difference between ourselves more
clearly than we see difference within ourselves because we have
flattened out the incongruous internal characteristics to create a
sharply defined identity to distinguish ourselves from others. Trinh
says, "Hegemony works at leveling out differences and at standard-
izing contexts and expectations in the smallest details of our daily
lives" (930).

Trinh's angle is to switch perspective and see oneself and others
as possessing a sea of differences and samenesses that are always
contextual and interdependent. With Trinh's shift in perspective,
we may begin to recreate difference as issue-focused rather than
identity-focused. We may, for instance, identify with others on
some issues (roles of women, importance of slowing climate change,
etc.) regardless of our racial or gendered or national identities. If
we think, for a moment, of the issues in which we join others as
more important than the issues that separate us, we are less likely to
see differences as either resolvable or incommensurable, but rather
temporally separate, depending on the issue. Taking a similar approach, Trinh sees interdependence as more creative than what she
calls "mutual enslavement" (932). With permeable identities we are
not so focused on ourselves and others as separate entities; rather
we are focused on the configuration of needs and desires and qualities on the table between us. Some of these we share, and they associate us. Some we don't share. From this perspective, difference is
"recreated" as issue-based rather than ontology-based, and identity
politics is put into question.

What might political practices look like if differences are issue-
focused, rather than identity-focused? Amie Macdonald and Susan
Sánchez-Casal try to answer that from a pedagogical perspective in
their edited collection titled *Twenty-First-Century Feminist Classrooms: Pedagogies of Identity and Difference* (2002). Macdonald and
Sánchez-Casal propose a restructuring of the epistemic framework

of the classroom from identity markers such as race and class to "communities of meaning" that enact collective knowledge making by allying students around issues and encouraging the shifting of bonds throughout the academic term, based on various shared experiences (11). This epistemic restructuring places the issue of identity in a context of hybridity, instability, and change—encouraging coalition rather than identity politics.[37] This focus on the temporary coalitions of provisional identities—issue by issue—changes the notion of "decentered" authority to what Bruffee has called "polycentric authority." Going back to 1971, Bruffee argued for collaborative learning as promoting collective authority gained by students in opposition to the teacher. At the same time, Elbow promoted decentering teacher authority. Macdonald and Sánchez-Casal, like Bruffee, distance themselves from the decentering of the teacher. But rather than focusing on the collective authority of undifferentiated students resisting teacher authority, as does Bruffee, Macdonald and Sánchez-Casal see students as forming and reforming group identities on the basis of provisional alliances. In other words, students can be divided into groups based on an interest in sustainability or class privilege, or an interest in marriage equality, regardless of conventional identity markers such as race, gender, sexuality, and disability. In what follows, I discuss three articles in Macdonald and Sánchez-Casal's collection that outline specific classroom activities that encourage rhetorical power based on alliances among students.

In her article "Representation, Entitlement, and Voyeurism: Teaching across Difference," Melanie Kaye/Kantrowitz uses a number of conventional feminist pedagogical strategies such as group work, a focus on the individual student, and deft teacher facilitation. Significant to her discussion is the way she offers students a way out of the limitations of identity. Students come with a felt sense of "essentialist" identity (I am a white woman; I am [not] a racist; I am [not] homophobic). She invites them to separate identity from behavior. The question isn't whether someone is or isn't homophobic in some socially constructed essentialist way. "Rather it's *did X or Y commit an act that objectively speaking strengthens rac-*

ism?" (291). Did you use a word that could strengthen racism? Did you refuse to attend a gay wedding because it was gay? She explains that "encircling the language or behavior allows for change; no one *has* to repeat the offensive act" (287). Kaye/Kantrowitz explains that "identity is not a fixed commodity but a process in which [a person] participates, consciously or not" (286). In other words, what is the history of an issue and what is my participation in that history? These strategies of shifting perspective allow students to see themselves as part of a larger social structure. "For traditional age students," Kaye/Kantrowitz says, who are "often most interested in the self, the course's emphasis on situating the self in the context that makes said self possible can feel like a guilt trip" (285). Some students are paralyzed by guilt; others feel anger or blame. The way out of those unproductive emotional states is, again, to focus on issues, not people, and to move toward multiple, flexible alignments and alliances over various issues. Depending on what the issue is, Kaye/Kantrowitz divides students into appropriate identities— gender, sexuality, class, and nation with the goal that those students "at least recognize that someone can be privileged along one axis and subordinated along another" (291).

> [I]n the social justice classroom the students' attitudes and experiences are part of our texts . . . . For the instructor, finding the delicate balance between supporting the anger while keeping the classroom a safe place takes skill, tact, time, and attention to group process, including figuring out when students need to meet in small groups and divided according to what logic. (288)

In this classroom practice, the teacher must exercise authority to negotiate social relations in the classroom.

Kaye/Kantrowitz desires a resuscitation of the relationship between theory and practice that women's studies once represented, the kind of work that Schniedewind and Shrewsbury introduced. She concludes with this statement: "What's needed is a post-post-modernism to move beyond fragmented identities, to rebuild the bridges between theoretical and practical work that characterized the best of early women's studies" (295). Kaye/Kantrowitz's work contributes to twenty-first-century feminist pedagogy the model of a teacher as a strong facilitator, a flexible designer of classroom dynamics, and a mediator of emotions. She offers students the knowledge and the emotional tools they need to become conscious of their impact on the world in order to use their various axes of privilege toward social justice.

Betty Sasaki's priorities are similar to Kaye/Kantrowitz's in that she sees historical awareness as key to students' learning to complicate identity, and she is also interested in social justice as the product. Although appreciating the attempt of twentieth-century feminists to allow students freedom of expression in the classroom, Sasaki is concerned about the impact of that model when it does not address levels of power and simultaneously undercuts the authority of the teacher. Sasaki states:

> A truly transformative feminist pedagogy must strategically and actively engage the multiple relationships of power that come into play in any classroom. It must move critically beyond mere gestures of equality and inclusiveness by examining the historical, cultural, and political differences both within and among members of a given community that, when they remain unrecognized, render such well-meaning gestures meaningless. (46)

In concrete terms of classroom practice, Sasaki asks students to explore issues of power and identity collectively, in interaction with their own and others' histories. Students in groups accomplish two tasks: (1) to research a history of their college and (2) to simultaneously research a history of their families from the date that the college was founded. The divergences among the college histories are then examined in relation to the personal/familial histories. It becomes apparent that individual student perspectives and relationships with the institution differ from others as they are built on their own familial and cultural histories.

Sasaki's project involves students' historicizing experience itself, very much in line with Dewey's thought in *Experience and Educa-*

tion. Students make a shift in perspective not only within themselves, but also in the way they see others (46–47). Whiteness is defamiliarized when students take it beyond personal background and experience, and historicize it. White students are invited into the double consciousness that nonwhite students in the United States are born into. This project, however, is just as important for nonwhite as for white students, for when they join together to protest administrative policy, for instance, they are coming with a deep well of knowledge and experience that puts them in a strong rhetorical position.

The issue of "what is racist" becomes seen as the intersectionality of hierarchized structures rather than a matter of blame, and a "pedagogy of coalition" is grounded not so much in "maintaining consensus" as in forming alliances, however uneasy they might be, both internally, within ourselves, and externally, with others. In this way, the central question becomes not just about having a voice, but "the sort of voice one comes to have as the result of one's location both as an individual and as part of collectives" (Mohanty 216). Sasaki says that part of the problem of relying on identity politics is that they mistake the visual (race, gender) with the ideological or experiential. An Asian American woman who teaches Spanish, Sasaki notes how when racial tension rose at her institution as a result of the Rodney King beating, an administrator expected her, as a woman of color in her second year at the university, to be part of the solution. "Given my gender, my biraciality, my heterosexuality, my working-class background, my institutional status as an untenured faculty member, my occupational status as a teacher of Spanish, from where did I speak?" (44). Sasaki's personal experience points out the misunderstandings that can result from our having expectations of a person based on one subject position, or as Krista Ratcliffe pointed out in responding to an earlier draft of this chapter, "Maybe it's more than a misunderstanding. Maybe it's a structure of white discourse . . . that is, a nonproductive white move of making nonwhites responsible for their own situations (while ignoring whites' implication or the structural dimension of the racism)." The reality of multiple subject positions is that they are neither separate nor equal, and their significance in one particular moment is bound by the power structures interpolated in the context.

It is exactly this issue that Sasaki's assignment implicitly elicits. Having done the historical research and experienced various alliances with classmates, what can the "individual" mean to students without the collective? How is the notion of individuality complicated by the students' emerging awareness of their family's history as it stacks up against the history of the institution in which they are being educated? They may gradually learn the complexity of identity, rather than facing their own culpability head-on and feeling guilt and anger.

Sasaki's work contributes to a twenty-first-century feminist-pedagogy model of the teacher as the facilitator of knowledge that students discover through research and create through interaction with peers. The authority structure in Sasaki's classroom makes hierarchy clear; her classroom is not a "democracy." Like Dewey's, Bruffee's, and Schniedewind's pedagogy, her class is meant to prepare students for democratic participation. Sasaki's goal is for students to understand levels of power and the material conditions that create it and maintain it. She challenges her students to place themselves and others in a historical context that is informed by careful research and discussion so that they emerge with the knowledge and tools to make a positive impact on their world, rather than being unconsciously controlled by forces they don't even know exist.

Similar to Kaye/Kantrowitz's and Sasaki's, Allison Dorsey's piece in *Twenty-First-Century Feminist Classrooms* implies a need for (1) less knee-jerk decentered teacher authority, and (2) much more attention to context. Her essay is titled "'white girls' and 'Strong Black Women': Reflections on a Decade of Teaching Black History at Predominantly White Institutions (PWIs)." Her most significant contribution is that she contextualizes the usefulness of "decentered authority." Arguments against teacher authority, for example, do not necessarily apply to working-class black female teachers like her. To "decenter" authority could yield to or reinforce the stereotypes the students, as mostly privileged white individuals, bring to the class. Her goal is to denaturalize *their* privilege. Dorsey asks, don't some subject positions need to be decentered and some brought to the center, depending on current structures of power?

Not considering the context of a particular pedagogical move is an example of the limitations of what Dorsey calls social construction "lite"—social construction without history. For instance, students may understand race as socially constructed and conclude that therefore it's not "real," thus neglecting to attend to the material conditions that produced the social construction. Dorsey states, "They do not grasp the limitations placed on actual human lives in the moment when race, or gender, or class is being constructed. Rather they latch on to the lyricism of the language and indulge in high-toned discussions of 'essentialist' thinking" (212–13). Social construction lite supports students' desire to remain in denial about painful historical realities (214).[38]

Dorsey critiques feminist pedagogy from the "mammy" perspective and the unreconstructed nurturing that her metaphor implies. All the emotional work associated with a "family" model, she says, is not appropriate; it can even be dysfunctional. Rather, she uses progressive pedagogical techniques such as dialectical journaling, life narratives, and student-centered discussion to bring students into an understanding of their positions in the social/political structures of power. She introduces her classes with a discussion of the importance of viewing the past "with a lens broader than one's personal life story" (216).

Dorsey redefines nurturing to mean something closer to traditional mentoring: to "encourage independent thought, help [students] improve academic skills, perhaps even guide them toward graduate programs that fit their talents." A teacher must possess the authority to be critical so that students are properly prepared for rigorous intellectual work. "Those students," she says, "who are accustomed to being rewarded simply for speaking are often startled by my pedagogical choice to challenge speech that is uninformed by the reading and/or thin analytically." Dorsey expects students to make claims based on persuasive arguments grounded in strong evidence (216). She uses "counter factual exercises" to introduce students to the complexities of history. For example, "What would have had to happen in order for [X] to have been successful?" Students are given roles and asked to research alternative decisions that might have been made (219). Sympathy and guilt are unproductive. According to Dorsey, "The key is to help students see the selfhood of all historical actors and see all such actors (including themselves) as both oppressors and oppressed" (224–25). This kind of careful research and understanding of the complexity of responsibility can provide the foundation for social change.

Dorsey is pessimistic about notions of classroom "community." Although she sees it as desirable, she also sees it as rare, a sense of connectedness that depends partly on luck and "must be made and remade in a thousand small ways each day" (217). And only with that connectedness can there be "safety." Further, community in the classroom doesn't necessarily translate to action outside the classroom, out of the context in which it occurred. Although skeptical of the notion of classroom community, Dorsey uses democratic structures in her classroom—including and perhaps emphasizing extracurricular consciousness-raising groups and involvement in campus activities to promote race consciousness. She particularly encourages black women across campus to engage with one another in building community. She says that they must lose the strong black woman stereotype and embrace their own and others' vulnerabilities. She explains, "I regularly encourage college-age black women to organize themselves into consciousness raising groups in which they can create community—plan activities, get involved with campus politics, but most importantly talk, share, and learn to trust one another with their fears" (220). This genuine community, according to Dorsey, goes beyond the classroom community that is narrowly built on teacher-initiated provisional alliances.

Dorsey is writing from her own situation as a black woman who teaches black history to white students. She believes in feminist pedagogy, she believes in teaching across difference, and, most important, she directly addresses the prevalent assumption of many progressive teachers that the teacher's power is the only power in the room that needs to be "decentered." She is engaging well be-

yond social construction "lite" when she exemplifies the importance of contextualizing power relations in particular classrooms to
determine which power should be "decentered."

Twenty-First-Century Feminist Classrooms offers versions of collaborative learning that go much further than does late-twentieth-
century collaborative pedagogy toward the Deweyan goal of historicizing practice. And they transcend both previous collaborative
learning and Dewey in their approaches to difference—freeing
the body to signify more than one subject position. In short, the
authority of knowledge is reconfigured from a decentered teacher
power or a collective student power to a complex notion of power
that involves multiple subject positions that coalesce differently depending on the issue and context.

The value of Schniedewind's work is her careful attention to
practice. She offers teachers specific steps for students to replace ineffective classroom behavior with the skills of agential change. We
need these steps. Too often, pedagogical articles give short shrift to
praxis, relying on the sophistication of discourse to play the transgressive role. The third-wave feminist pedagogies I discuss in this
chapter offer startlingly insightful approaches to activist pedagogy
based on an understanding of identity as fluid but not without
agency, particularly when in provisional alliance with others. Wor-
rying less about how to resolve differences, these teachers are finding ways to compose differences in new ways that can help students
feel less stifled by or accountable to identity labels and more open
to historicizing their experiences in relation to the material conditions of systemic oppression.

6

The Writing Center

PEER TUTORING IN WRITING CENTERS, COUNTED BY some to be the source of collaborative learning "at the beginning of the field," is now at the cutting edge of the discipline because of its transnational and international work. At the same time, emerging uses of technology are redefining the traditional essay genre. In some sense this empowers tutors to engage with new forms of writing familiar to students, and in another sense it is widening the gap between those who have access to the technology and those who don't.

In this chapter I argue that the writing center functions as both the site of origin of collaborative learning in the 1970s and the site of technological and transnational boundary crossing in collaborative learning now. First I will sketch a history of writing centers from a pragmatist perspective. Next I address the question "Who are the students?" Then I will look at the expansion of peer tutoring into European contexts, and finally I show how developments in technology have affected work in writing centers.

HISTORY

Given its historical connection to open admissions in the CUNY system, the writing center is arguably the origin of the late-1970s version of collaborative learning that helped create the field of rhetoric and composition as we know it today. The writing center itself, sans collaboration, began much earlier, as Neal Lerner demonstrates in *The Idea of a Writing Laboratory*. Lerner sees Helen Parkhurst's Dalton Plan in the 1920s as the first writing lab since it individualized student instruction in a resource-rich setting with the teacher as an occasional consultant to students who are working through a series of exercises on their own (see Parkhurst). Lerner notes that there are other references to writing labs or clinics, or, in one case, hospitals, but he quotes Christina Murphy, Joe Law, and Steve Sherwood, who describe Parkhurst's plan as the "central text and philosophy from which much writing center theory and practice derive" (31). Elizabeth Boquet's delineation of the writing center's history focuses on the scholarship of the writing center and shows a similar chronology. For both Lerner and Boquet, the early writing labs were based on student-centered methods but not necessarily collaborative learning, or the notion of students working together as peers. The most influential work that puts peer relationships at the heart of the writing center is Kenneth Bruffee's.

As a writing program administrator and writing center director, Bruffee helped found the Council of Writing Program Administration and its journal *WPA*. The writing center directors he taught at his summer institutes for training peer tutors were from all across the country. A condition of acceptance into the program was a commitment from the writing center directors' institutions to set up peer-tutor training programs upon their return. A special issue of *Writing Center Journal*, published in 2008, details the work of the institute and its effects by some of the participants themselves. Among them, Harvey Kail has been the most influential by beginning an ongoing longitudinal study in 1984 called the Peer Writing Tutor Alumni Research Project. The project provides empirical evidence for Bruffee's initial claims that peer-tutor training using collaborative methods benefits tutors at least as much as it benefits tutees. In 1984 Kail helped found the National Conference on Peer Tutoring in Writing (NCPTW), which is an organization of peer tutors. Undergraduate students regularly come to conferences, present papers, and engage in intellectual exchange with leaders in the field and peer tutors from other institutions. Through the NCPTW, the tutors themselves have a national/international community of peers and are thus participating professionally as undergraduates.

Since the inception and dissemination of Bruffee's program, regional, national, and most recently international organizations have provided an intellectual home for writing-center directors, peer tutors, and those interested in promoting academic writing through various collaborations. Scholarship on collaborative learning in writing centers since 2000 has focused on broadening definitions of students and of writing itself. New media have sparked challenges and innovations and critical debates in the writing center community.

IDENTITY: WHO ARE THE STUDENTS?

In the writing center at Brooklyn College in the early 1970s, the student tutees were a diverse group that would not previously have been accepted to college, but, beyond Mina Shaughnessy's book, which assumes an African American population of students, we don't hear much about the students themselves. In fact Bruffee's interest soon shifted from the student tutees to the student tutors, who were ostensibly those who would have been accepted even before open admissions began. As diversity among students has become more apparent in the context of identity politics, scholars are talking about the identities of the tutees and their impact on the collaborative nature of peer tutoring. The varieties of at-risk students have broadened with new student populations entering the system in the twenty-first century, Harry C. Denny says, in his book *Facing the Center: Toward an Identity Politics of One-To-One Mentoring*. This population includes disabled students, L2+ students, LGBTQ students, and students with other diverse issues. Denny notes that the affluent white student is not really a peer of the student he or she may tutor, and thus may unconsciously participate in the othering of the tutees, including poor and immigrant and EFL students (120). The antidote to that, says Denny, is for tutors to be connected to the community outside the university and committed to helping students bring their home identities into play with their emerging academic identities. Denny promotes the writing center as a site of activism (7). To ground his vision of tutoring as a community-based project, he draws on Antonio Gramsci's theory of the organic intellectual (22, 44) and Pierre Bourdieu's analyses of the role of cultural capital and communities of meaning (69). The system should always be interrogated, Denny argues. We should ask ourselves what kinds of oppression we are complicit with, perhaps unconsciously (8). Tutor training then must include an analysis of the cultural and economic environment that students inhabit and the assumptions tutors make about their tutees and themselves. Though Bruffee worked against the idea of tutors as "little teachers," warning that a hierarchical relationship in the mind of the tutor would undermine the relationship, he seemed to see the peer-tutor role as a set of behaviors rather than as a perhaps unconscious attitude, as Denny's work suggests it is.

A significant student identification in twenty-first-century tutoring is that of the international student. John Trimbur (along with Bruce Horner and Paul Matsuda in other contexts) critiques the prevalent assumption in US composition studies that our students' first language is English. A special issue of the *Writing Center Journal* in 2010 includes a reprint of Trimbur's 2000 article "Multiliteracies, Social Futures, and Writing Centers," which advocates extending tutoring services to languages other than English. Like Denny, Trimbur emphasizes the importance of the students' home communities. He is interested in "redistributing the means of communication" by bringing writing-center work into local communities (89). An article by Gail Okawa et al. in the same issue shows how their institutions have addressed multilingual students. Their writing centers' missions have switched from a goal of literacy to one of multiliteracy. Students and tutors together participate in the common goal of multiliteracy, rather than attempting to move students from their home languages and dialects to a "standard" notion of literacy. Told through the voices of tutors, their piece posits that collaboration is key to the bilingual or bidialectal function of writing centers.

Combining Trimbur's and Okawa and her colleagues' intention to decenter the United States in writing center practice and Denny's advocacy of activism, Anis Bawarshi and Stephanie Pelkowski use the metaphor of code switching to reframe the writing center as a postcolonial site. They propose to replace the writing center's process approach with a critical approach that involves students' taking on a mestizo identity to understand both US academic codes and the cultural groundings of their own nations' codes. In this model students must understand the political position to which they have been assigned and take a strategic position of agency within that structure. Bawarshi and Pelkowski's reframing of the mission of the writing center removes hierarchy as even a temptation. What makes this tutoring activist is that an analysis of the relationship between rhetoric and power is at the heart of the method.

COLLABORATIVE WRITING CENTERS
OUTSIDE THE UNITED STATES

Until the twenty-first century, the writing center was a US phenomenon, but with the development of writing instruction in the vernacular in other countries, and with the United States as an initial model, the European Writing Center Association was founded in 2000. Its founding as a regional affiliate of the US-based National Writing Centers Association prompted a name change to the International Writing Centers Association (IWSA).[39] There are many differences among writing centers in different countries, all which come out of the countries' cultural traditions and situational needs. I will describe two: the community-based Leipzig Project and the online Belgian Calliope.

Gerd Bräuer's Leipzig Project is an example of the kind of community-based project that Denny and Trimbur suggest. Based on the tenets of "[training] the trainer" and "discursive mobility," Bräuer's mission for the writing center is to melt the boundaries between the university and local communities (9). He likens the work to the "community gardens" project in Lincoln, Nebraska, and he sees it as responding to the heightened mobility of the twenty-first century. The Leipzig Project extends literacy to new immigrants, and it teaches affluent young people about the history and needs of the poorer people in the community who are less geographically mobile than they. Bräuer acknowledges the influence of John Dewey. He sees each part of the community as symbiotically, reciprocally influencing the others. In his project, the stakeholders include the writing center at the University of Education in Freiburg, the

City Library of Leipzig, the local community college, the University of Leipzig, the local schools, and volunteer-based literacy initiatives (10).

Following Dewey, Bräuer's goal is to educate the citizens of Leipzig, an economically failing city, in participatory democracy so they can govern their own lives. "Training the tutors" is the first leg of the program. "Discursive mobility" is the second. Bräuer trains the tutors at the university, who then train high-school tutors, who take literacy skills to their communities. Tutors develop skills of "discursive mobility" by modifying the system at each step to better meet local needs. *Discursive mobility* is a term adapted from migration studies to apply to writing pedagogy: "the ability to move, as needed, between different knowledge communities and gather information necessary for one's own personal development." Bräuer sees this as a catalyst for creativity at each point, not for the individual only, but for the communities affected by his or her mobility (11). Bräuer argues that discursive mobility is a key competency in the twenty-first century. His mission responds to the history of stasis in Eastern Europe, during which citizens were permitted very little movement—geographically, economically, or socially.

Bräuer reconceives the writing center as a way to teach discursive mobility, to prepare citizens to move among various discourse communities. His vision involves the writing center at the core of local democratic and educational enrichment, which if duplicated across the country could lead to economic and democratic development of the former East Germany. It could also promote a workable alternative to the more familiar authoritarian style of working together, which Bräuer hopes to replace. Thus Bräuer's interest in the interactions of people with one another, the "local we," functions as a reformist form of activism, much as Dewey envisioned education in the early twentieth century.

Calliope, an online writing center based at the University of Antwerp in Belgium, is at the other end of the spectrum from Bräuer's Leipzig Project. It is designed specifically for academic writing. As Bräuer's mission is to bring "discursive mobility" to the community, Calliope prepares university students for specific careers.

The front page of the Calliope website prompts the viewer to select one of three languages—Dutch, English, or French—the official languages of Belgium. The center is discipline-based, unlike US online writing centers such as Purdue's OWL. According to Lisbeth Opdenacker and Luuk Van Waes, this is because of the "early specialization" of schools in Europe, in which students begin work in their majors immediately upon entering college (248). Its purpose, then, can be compared to Writing Across the Curriculum or Writing in the Disciplines programs in the United States. Calliope promotes the concept that students need to learn how to function as writers in a particular field using the authoritative expertise of their teachers. Although it is deeply collaborative, the site is not "student-centered" in the way US writing centers addressing more general rhetorical concerns are.

Calliope's mission is based on "blended learning," in which traditional class meetings are supplemented by two uses of Calliope: one for guided help with assignments and the other for structured peer interaction, which is heavily based on collaborative feedback methods (248–49). It is also structured impeccably using software such as Textpert and Escribamos to strictly organize the feedback loop (248). Students are given clear directions and guidelines and are put into interaction with one another to review others' work through several revisions. It is also necessary for students to engage in self-exploration to discover their own writing styles. Calliope's staff gives as much attention to individual exploration as they do to structured peer feedback.

Calliope's striking contrast with the Leipzig Project underlines the importance of context. In Calliope the authority of knowledge is validated by disciplines and experts. In Leipzig, knowledge is uncertain, therefore possibly democratic, much like the way it was articulated by pragmatist philosophers after the US Civil War. In Calliope, social relations or peer-to-peer interactions are highly regulated and organized. Bräuer's discursive mobility invites change from step to step. Tutors are asked to make changes to what they've been taught as they are confronted with a new audience. Authority is negotiable in Leipzig. Authority is embedded in software created by experts in Antwerp. The differences I am noticing between the two sites are the first steps in the kind of analysis I am advocating in this book. The next step is curiosity. What do I need to know about Antwerp to make sense of this comparison? What more do I need to know about Leipzig? How will my further understanding of both situations help me to understand the variables of knowledge, power, and social relations embedded, but invisible to me, in my own structures of work?

I will end this section with Christiane Donahue, who argues in "'Internationalization' and Composition Studies: Reorienting the Discourse" that although the European academic writing movement has borrowed much from US writing instruction, it is a mistake for us to think of ourselves as the world experts. We have much to learn from European writing instruction. And the work in the International Writing Centers Association is leading the field.

DIGITAL TECHNOLOGY

As literacies expanded from print to the electronic word, tutors faced the challenges of a new technology. At first, debate centered on whether or how composing on a computer changed the writing process. Jeanne Luchte, in "Computer Programs in the Writing Center: A Bibliographic Essay," summarizes the then-current scholarship and software on each stage of the writing process. Early forms of the Daedalus Group's InterChange, in fact, adapted some of Maxine Hairston's and Kenneth Bruffee's guidelines for peer criticism into software. Many writing centers were eventually equipped with computers, leading to the concept of an "online writing center." Scholarship on computer-mediated writing centers has taken two directions: (a) online writing centers and (b) the redefinition of "text."

Sam Racine, Denise Dilworth, and Lee-Ann Kastman Breuch have demonstrated that online writing centers require a sophisticated rhetorical use of collaborative principles in both use and design. They began their research with this question: How might we involve the audience of an online writing center in the design and structure of the process? They used a method called "participatory design," which relies on users' perspectives and their participation in the design (61–62).[40] The users in their case were students, teachers, and Web designers (60, 65). They make up what James Porter terms a *local we,* a group bound by affiliations, conventions, discipline, or common interests—not necessarily by geographical space (64). The concept of a "local we" helped the researchers frame the stakeholders in a collaborative framework. They tested the importance of power differentials among the three groups by conducting surveys and focus groups and experimenting with various levels of teacher presence (65). They found, for example, that when teachers left the room when surveys were administered, the answers were more complete (69). Their study points to implications of collaborative learning taken to an institutional and research level. Collaborative learning is not only a classroom pedagogy; it is also a way to think through larger structures in the way academic learning is imagined.

One of the ways that academic writing has been reimagined is in the definition of a text. What is the tutor's role when students bring multimodal texts into the writing center? The paper essay is no longer the default, contends Jackie Grutsch McKinney in "New Media Matters: Tutoring in the Late Age of Print" (33). She combines the definitions of new media of Anne Wysocki, Cynthia Selfe, and Cheryl Ball to say that they "show a range of texts that are 'new' in significant ways: (1) their digital-ness; (2) their conscious materiality or form; (3) their multimodality; and/or (4) their rhetorical means" (31).[41]

Tutors teaching new media will radically change conventional tutoring practices, says McKinney (36). Table 6.1 illustrates her perspective on these changes. How does McKinney's argument fit with the prevailing assumption that writing centers are based on collaborative methods? How does she answer those who at some level fear that they don't know enough to train tutors in new media? Writing centers have never been about expertise, she answers, but rather about talk between tutors (49). The larger question for me is the distance between the cutting edge and what Selfe calls the ragged edge. How do we begin to address the issue of access?

Table 6.1. McKinney's Comparison of Last-Century and Contemporary Tutoring Practices (48)

Twentieth-Century Tutoring	Twenty-First-Century Tutoring
Read aloud	Talk aloud
Getting beyond the text	Interacting with the text
Zoomed in: talk about words	Zoomed out: talk about whole

I have shown how writing centers grew out of the civil rights activism of the early 1970s in New York City. Current historical situations for writing centers include the increased numbers of at-risk students of various identities, the population explosion of international students entering US colleges and universities, the emergence of writing centers in Europe after the breakup of the Soviet Union, and the cultural shift from print text to communication in new media. In Chapter 7, I will address the intersection of classroom collaboration and technology.

7

Computer-Mediated Collaboration

IN THIS CHAPTER, I ARGUE THAT COMPUTER-MEDIATED collaboration, the history and conception of which is solidly connected to Deweyan/Bruffeean theory and practice, expanded the possibilities of collaborative learning to represent the social construction of knowledge. I do not demonstrate a comprehensive view of the relationship between Deweyan collaborative principles and the infinitely various forms of work and play in cyberspace. And I should point out that there are parallel sites of early collaborative practices that had their own origins—most notably Cynthia Selfe and Dickie Selfe's groundbreaking work at Michigan Technological University. The scope of my work, however, is limited to collaborative practice in two periods—the emergence of networked classrooms and the Daedalus Group at the University of Texas at Austin in the late 1980s and the current development of wiki pedagogy. An analysis of knowledge, power, and social relations in the scholarships of both networked classrooms and wiki pedagogy can show how these are negotiated as collaborative learning adapts to new technologies. These practices are significant in that they both participate in a passionate embrace of democratic reform followed by skepticism, and then they are forgotten, only to be independently renewed in a different historical situation.

NETWORKED COMPUTER CLASSROOMS
Computer-mediated pedagogy in networked computer classrooms represented a watershed in collaborative learning not seen since Kenneth Bruffee's initial work in 1971. In 1984, a progressive College of Liberal Arts dean named Sheldon Ekland-Olson ordered

computers for two classrooms in the Department of English at the University of Texas at Austin. Speaking from my own experience, I didn't get the sense that they were requested; they just showed up. No one on the faculty was prepared to address the situation immediately, although Lester Faigley may be able to tell a different story. A group of graduate students who became the staff of the Computer Writing and Research Lab (CWRL) set about trying to figure out what to do with them. At first, they worked on developing interactive software that students could use individually, much like a handbook. After they learned at a conference about Bruffee's use of social-constructionist theory and practice, however, their goals shifted. I had introduced Bruffee's textbook into the curriculum as an "alternate text," and I was familiar with his scholarly work; I gave them print copies of all his articles not available in the library. They eventually created a company, Daedalus, to create software for networked computers in English studies before the advent of the Web. Founding Daedalus members such as Fred Kemp, Wayne Butler, Valerie Balester, and Joyce Locke Carter designed interactive software based on a combination of Bruffee's peer critiques and Maxine Hairston's peer-critique guidelines. When the computers were networked, versions of synchronous communication (such as MOOs) created opportunities for students to "speak" directly to others in the class, in some cases using pseudonyms.[42]

The computer-mediated software that came out of this collaboration is called the Daedalus Integrated Writing Environment, or DIWE (pronounced *dee*-wee).[43] Bruffee's work was significant in the design of DIWE, and in that way he influenced the social direction of computer-mediated instruction. By connecting computers via local area networks, Daedalus featured a collaborative synchronous conference module called InterChange (IC) that for the first time allowed the class to participate in discussions online in real time. Transcripts of the discussions were made available for interpretation, critique, and fodder for invention in the writing process. InterChange opened up the possibilities of collaborative learning at a time when social construction was a new theory and, for many of us, had changed our perceptions of our jobs as educators.

The teacher accustomed to collaborative practice did not have to be talked into the advantages of "decentered" teacher authority. But what Bruffee and feminist pedagogy had valued was the carefully designed reconstruction of power much in line with Dewey's pedagogical goals for an expansion of democratic practices. Whereas face-to-face collaboration offers teachers the opportunity to either complicate or dismiss a hierarchical teacher role, the technology of networked synchronous discussions created a sudden, dramatic shift in the teacher's sense of authority. The teacher was suddenly decentered whether he or she wanted to be or not, becoming just one more typist in the mad rush to "speak," and in an environment in which everyone was typing at the same time and classroom conversational etiquette was suddenly extinct. My early experience with new TAs in synchronous classroom discussion was chaotic. TAs who had been polite and productive in the classroom suddenly took pseudonyms and the subject positions of rebellion and anarchy. One student came out as transgender (in the early 1990s). They took my calm reaction as a sign they could talk to me after class. It was exhilarating, while at the same time I had no idea what my responsibility was as a teacher in such an environment. Furthermore, when I took the role of a student in a colleague's class, I experienced an irrepressible desire to make trouble. Scholarly conversation on the topic of power in networked classrooms moved from how much responsibility the teacher should assume in constructing student relationships in the classroom to how or whether discursive student relationships running wild could be controlled by a suddenly powerless teacher. Several approaches were developed to address the issues of authority and social relations.

Beth Kolko created a task that asked students to analyze their individual responsibilities in synchronous discussions. She used Bruffeean collaborative activities to foreground the cultural studies problematic of subjective agency, articulating the problem of subjectivity by posing questions "that take issue with the ways in which the society constructs individuals," that focus on "the tension between the determined subject and the determining individual—the agent" (33). She raised her students' awareness through collaborative practices in which they learned to treat one another's utterances and writing as worthy of citation. As with Bruffee and Daedalus, students collaborated in "the intellectual process of brainstorming, refining, and challenging arguments" (34). Thus Kolko's cultural studies approach brought collaborative practice and critical consciousness of the production of knowledge into dialectical relation.

Laurie George attempted to resuscitate a hierarchical teacher role. In the provocatively titled "Taking Women Professors Seriously: Female Authority in the Computerized Classroom," George posited first that a decentered, collaborative teaching style was the norm, as evidenced by her teaching space at the New York Institute of Technology, which promoted collaboration in its architecture, spacing, and lighting. In synchronous networked discussions, however, female teachers had to deal with the cultural tensions embodied in her (mostly male) students, for whom playful student chatter could often be seriously sexist, even toward the teacher. Noting a contradiction between the feminist pedagogical mission and the resulting sexist behavior on the part of the self-determining students, George claimed that the student "wilding" she observed enacted the patriarchal assumptions that a feminist classroom was meant to challenge. Because of this contradiction, George enacted what she perceived as masculinist authority behavior. Taking from Adrienne Rich the contention that women must use their authority, George didn't hesitate to "call" students on their sexist and racist language in a networked classroom, including making them read aloud their own comments in the transcript.

Other teachers addressed authority in the networked classroom by attending to the students' relations with one another. Rather than appropriate a masculinist form of leadership, as did George, Sara Pace first taught and then modeled appropriate behavior for her students. Pace suggested we teach students to use the same skills in computer-assisted discussion as we do in face-to-face conversation. Quoting Gail Stygall, she wrote: the "feminist teacher of composition who uses collaboration must also be willing to use her authority in the classroom to model a different kind of discourse for women students" (107). In her article "Feminist Pedagogy and Daedalus Online" Pace described her study comparing a face-to-face class with an online class.

Christyne A. Berzsenyi similarly took the approach of teaching students behavioral skills for online conversations. She did so by analyzing the transcripts of synchronous discussions with students, pointing to particular behaviors and their consequences. Berzsenyi developed an "interlocutor relationship continuum" (232). She and the students "coded" conversational utterances as agonistic (conflictual, competitive, rude), hierarchical (reporting, giving information or advice), dialectical (showing equal partnership), and empathic (giving praise or support). Instructors could use these transcripts and students' analyses of them to suggest behaviors appropriate for working toward a goal, whatever that might have been. Off-task behavior was obvious. Patterns became clear. Role-playing was useful (241). Berzsenyi hoped that her methods could create less agonistic, more negotiative discourse in the classroom and in the culture beyond schooling. Berzsenyi was interested in ethics. We are in a position to teach this behavior, said Berzsenyi, so we should do it.

As did Marilyn Cooper in "Postmodern Possibilities in Electronic Conversations," Berzsenyi posited a socially constructed, ever-shifting collaborative persona for synchronous computer conference (SCC) participants. And, like Cooper, she argued for students' individual responsibility. She went a step further, however, when she encouraged students to become aware of the power dynamics embedded in various chat discourses to recognize how interlocutor relationships are collaboratively constructed through discursive actions. These descriptions of interactions implied power dynamics that were both a characteristic and a consequence of their inter-relationships (231–32). Berzsenyi's tactics fit Dewey's criteria of interaction and continuity, and of teacher as architect, not spectator.

In a collaborative approach Carol Winkelmann tracked what happened when composing was defined as the singular product and process of the entire class. Winkelmann began with some assumptions that bore directly upon the question of the subject:

- that in the postmodernist, post-feminist digital era, identity ought to be seen as cyborg identity, which is by definition multiple, contradictory, and in dialectical relation to technology;
- that electronic literacy is rooted in collaborative work that is anarchic, nonhierarchical, and transformative; and
- that the resulting text will break the conventions of linear, academic texts.

To enact these assumptions, Winkelmann set up parameters for students that eschewed many of the usual decision-making roles of the instructor, placing all composing responsibility on students. The course readings immersed students in the discourse of computer textuality (Jay David Bolter's *Writing Space*) and cyberpunk literature and film. Students then took on various roles in relation to the emerging group identity. Here, the "group" was the whole class. Individuals clashed, cooperated, negotiated, and confronted individual difference, which led to a transformation of social relations and expanded individual subjectivity. Through this conflictual, fragmented process of writing as role-playing, students "found themselves-in-community" and performed literacy through "shifting identities, dependencies, and combinations." One result was that students spurned outside critique of their texts, suggesting a shift to a dispersed community-based authority, "earned by the development of expertise" (441).

Computer-mediated pedagogy—particularly synchronous discussion—clearly favors social relations, amplifying their importance. Teacher authority is easy to lose, difficult to maintain—clearly the opposite of the situation in previous collaborative pedagogies. In networked computer pedagogy, authority is a reciprocal relationship among, not between, students and teacher. In synchronous discussions, "teacher" and "students" begin to seem like unhelpful categories. Much of the initial excitement about the egalitarian promise and democratic potential of networked computer discourse was frankly utopian, and like the "no place" that is the derivation of that word, existed perhaps more in perception than in reality. Although the unruliness of synchronous conferencing was acknowledged early on, it was commonly seen as a discourse arena potentially blind to race, gender, ethnicity, and class power differentials. It did not take long, however, for corrective analyses to be published and integrated into the field's thinking. Among them were Susan Romano's widely cited "The Egalitarianism Narrative" and Faigley's "Achieved Utopia" chapter in his book *Fragments of Rationality*. Notably, both Romano and Faigley came out of the University of Texas at Austin, where the initial optimism had thrived. While students felt freer to express themselves in the networked sessions, closer scrutiny of the discourse revealed that denigrating language against minority populations was frequent.

While some instructor-researchers were disturbed by the flame-like tones, centrifugal force, and associational, rhizomatic growth of synchronous conferencing, others valued these same qualities as revealing elements of textuality often repressed in linear, logical, academically sanctioned writing. Anthony DiMatteo praised synchronous conferencing as a new text that defies resolution: "an unpredictable and unruly exchange of ideas creates an open-ended, forward moving discourse that wanders endlessly and which has deviation as its most persistent theme." What others criticized as "flaming," DiMatteo saw as a significant breakthrough to a truer view of discourse: "An obstreperous freeplay authorizes and sanctions real-time writing" (n.p.). In "A Class of Clowns," Christopher Holcomb saw his students' collaborative humor in Daedalus's InterChange as demonstrating competence in a new discourse venue. Albert Rouzie analyzed playful discourse in InterChange as, at times, "serio-ludic," combining playful and serious effects and motivations. Cooper disagreed with Faigley's analysis in *Fragments of Rationality* of an unruly classroom session, finding the students' subversions more ethical and less disturbing than Faigley did. Geoffrey Sirc and Tom Reynolds found that basic writers' refusal to play by the rules of collaborative group work in InterChange could be seen as a significant form of resistance leading to identification with a subcultural style.

Enter the World Wide Web and these particular conversations stopped, and others took their place. Fast forward thirty years to the next flowering of Bruffee-influenced electronic collaborative pedagogy, and you have the wiki.

THE WIKI

Frustration with the limitations of the Web for collaboration—basically the inability to alter any pages other than your own—led to the development of wikis, software that allows just such collaborative writing and editing. If the general trend is toward more dynamic sites that can change easily and often, online collaboration reached a new high with wiki software. Wikis are fully editable websites. Any user can both read and alter the content. Wiki software, originated by Wikipedia, enables students to respond directly to webtexts, helping to shape a text in the process of its publication, and wiki scholars are using collaborative learning to theorize their work. The emerging wiki discourse owes much to the pragmatism of Dewey, the contributions of Bruffee, the correctives of Trimbur, and the early egalitarian optimism of synchronous discussions on networked computers.

Wikis give students a chance to work individually and together to shape a single text and to have the process of writing staring them in the face. Whereas in earlier computer-mediated pedagogy the text (essay) was in the background of the foregrounded student discourse, in the wiki, the text regains a prominent position. Knowledge, authority, and social relations are collaborative in the wiki, perhaps the most fully realized representation of social construction yet. Adherents claim that wikis represent the social construction of knowledge most fully because the process is laid out on the page. Knowledge evolves as a gradual dialectic between multiple readers (one at a time) and a common text. The text is in a constant process of change, and the process is transparent to all involved. In most wikis, authority is polycentral, and the strongest relationship is between the various readers and the text. Social relations are virtual; people don't necessarily see each other, but they see each other's traces (history).

These abilities and the uses to which they are put in the classroom and the philosophy that inspires the use of the wiki contributes to pragmatist themes of democracy and socially constructed knowledge that have been a mainstay of various forms of collaborative pedagogy over the twentieth century. The cultural significance of the wiki is well penned by Robert Cummings in his introduction to his text *Wiki Writing: Collaborative Learning in the College Classroom,* coedited with Matt Barton:

> [T]his introduction hopes to show nonbelievers, the uninitiated, and wiki followers alike that the simple act of allowing a Web page to be edited by a reader—which is really all that a wiki does—has created a global transition to networked epistemology that affects most anyone who is concerned with knowledge acquisition, whether it is defined broadly, as the search for teleological ends, or narrowly, as the search for Chinese takeout. (2–3)

A description of Wikipedia might be helpful here. If you go to "Athens Lunatic Asylum," for instance, you will see that the menu at the top of the screen has five tabs: Article, Talk, Read, Edit, and History. The history tab enables users to look at a list of changes that have been made to the entry since its publication. The edit tab allows users to suggest changes themselves. The talk tab is a place where users can discuss the revisions. Wikipedia is a public forum. Classroom wikis function in a similar way. Before I get to the classroom wiki, though, I'm going to start with a description of Wikipedia, the encyclopedia.

Wikipedia

Wikipedia describes itself as a "multilingual, Web-based, free-content encyclopedia project supported by the Wikimedia Foundation and based on a model of openly editable content." Wikipedia's articles are linked with one another to offer more information on a particular topic or concept. Wikipedia is written collaboratively by largely anonymous Internet volunteers who write without pay. Anyone with Internet access can write and make changes to Wikipedia articles, except in limited cases where editing is restricted to prevent disruption or vandalism. Users can contribute anonymously, under pseudonyms, or, if they choose to, with their real identities.

The fundamental principles by which Wikipedia operates are the "five pillars," which the editors insist are not rules, but rather flexible guidelines. The attempt is to encourage people to add to Wikipedia, however much or little they know about the encyclopedia. I reproduce an abridged version below:

> *Wikipedia is an encyclopedia.* It is not a soapbox, an advertising platform, a vanity press, an experiment in anarchy or democracy, an indiscriminate collection of information, or a web directory. It is not a dictionary, a newspaper, or a collection of source documents.
>
> *Wikipedia is written from a neutral point of view.* We avoid advocacy and we characterize information and issues rather than debate them.
>
> *Wikipedia is free content that anyone can edit, use, modify, and distribute.* [There are exceptions.]
>
> *Editors should treat each other with respect and civility.*
>
> *Wikipedia does not have firm rules.* ("Wikipedia: Five Pillars")

Browsing Wikipedia can give you a quick idea of the range of quality of the articles (excellent and reliable to shabby and far-fetched), but also can provide a sense of the collaborative nature of knowledge.

James P. Purdy, in a *College Composition and Communication* article, "When the Tenets of Composition Go Public: A Study of Writing in Wikipedia," describes his study of three Wikipedia texts over a period of several years for the purpose of following the process of revision. Purdy's article shows the value of Wikipedia (and other similar electronic resources) in revealing the knowledge production that is hidden in other encyclopedias. He notes several ways in which Wikipedia differs from a traditional reference source.

Visitors to a page, Purdy notes, can click "history" to see the layers of revisions and click "edit this page" to begin a revision of their own. The original author doesn't have the last word (353). The "document mode" gives the current page; the "thread mode" gives the discussion about what's on the current page. The "citation" system is not hierarchical, as in academic work, but webbed and not based on traditionally understood expertise (357). "[R]esearch [is] based on production rather than mere critique" (365), information is not received efficiently, but is generative (365), and knowledge is provisional and temporary and subject to individuals' revision (366).

Wikipedia and the classroom wikis that followed it make up a new form of collaborative learning, one in which "consensus" doesn't even make sense, since no provisional agreement is reached, and no one has the last word. Interestingly, as Wikipedia has become more successful, it has introduced increased controls on the content so that recent changes made by users are quickly reviewed by editors and often deleted. This has improved the quality of the entries. Even though student writers might see their Wikipedia pieces deleted, the venue offers, through the thread mode, the ability to question an editor's decision, to possibly receive feedback from editors and other users, and to further collaborate on writing that might better meet the quality criteria and expectations of the Wikipedia staff. The relative speed of these exchanges makes the process logistically reasonable for a course, and it can provide students with a "real-world" sense of both collaboration and editorial authority. Instructors who would rather limit the process to the class community can set up wikis for their classes and limit access should they see fit. Teachers who use wikis in their classrooms fall into two categories: those who work directly with Wikipedia, and those who set up classroom wikis. I'll start with the scholarship in the first category, those teachers who organize their students to contribute to the public encyclopedia.

One way teachers use Wikipedia is to show students how the site represents the process of writing. Carra Leah Hood describes Wikipedia as a form of peer critique with a global audience. If we assign our students to compose Wikipedia entries, they ideally have that global audience. The pedagogy offers, in effect, a real-world experience. Hood says:

> Wikipedia becomes a container for writing. A singular, stable, identifiable author does not exist for Wikipedia entries; however, the wiki software retains authorial functions; the "history" tab lists contributors, those responsible for particular edits, and identifies their changes, a form of acknowledgment, while the "discussion" tab chronicles contributors' conversations on the way to consensus, a means to determine accountability, attribution, and reliability. ("Wikipedia in Composition")

This is collaborative experience beyond the peer critique. Students experience consequences, not grades. When critics of Wikipedia judge an entry disparagingly as incomplete or inaccurate, the judgment itself is a misunderstanding. They're not seeing a product; they're seeing a work in progress. Hood asks whether we should start thinking about grading final products as "rhetorically insufficient."

Matthew Vetter found that writing a Wikipedia entry can enable a class of composition students to meet traditional course outcomes. Students in Vetter's class submitted the new topic "Athens Lunatic Asylum" to Wikipedia editors and created a page as a term project. Although Vetter claims that the endeavor wasn't completely peer-collaborative (given the need to negotiate with the Wikipedia editors), he reports that the students' excitement, motivation, and conscientiousness was tangible. He asked the following research questions: (1) Can engaging students in online discourse—such as that made available by Wikipedia—fulfill traditional course competencies? (2) Does the encyclopedia actually provide opportunities, as suggested by Purdy and Hood, for students to learn about writing processes and to study and engage in writing as a social-collaborative act? (3) How does the presence of online audiences influence student writing? (4) Do students respond positively or negatively to this type of pedagogy? Vetter's results were based on three kinds of student response: a survey that included both short-answer questions and discursive responses, and a reflective paper. He found overwhelmingly positive responses to the questions. Three themes emerged in the discursive responses. Students discovered writing as a social experience with a wider audience than they were accustomed to. They learned to research, retrieve sources, and incorporate their research into their texts. And they maintained that they improved in general writing skills, style, and tone. In the reflective papers, four major themes emerged that demonstrate student growth in understanding: (1) textual authority and ethos, (2) writing as a social/collaborative act, (3) the rhetorical impact of audience, and (4) writing processes. Vetter notes in his discussion that "the encyclopedia is a manifestation of epistemology in transition" ("Composing").

Classroom Wikis

Now that I have addressed pedagogy in which students work directly with Wikipedia, I will turn to those who set up classroom wikis.[44] But first, a warning. In "What Was a Wiki, and Why Do I Care? A Short and Usable History of Wikis," Robert Cummings warns against conflating the wiki with the more familiar Wikipedia. Although the creation of Wikipedia is essential to the history of the wiki, he says, there are ways in which other wikis are different: they are not encyclopedias, so they are not directly in the business of creating knowledge, and they do not have the public stature and therefore scrutiny that Wikipedia does (3–4).[45] Because of its scope and its size and responsibility, it is no longer, he says, completely open-source (4).

The very idea of a wiki implies that knowledge is a fragmented, socially constructed process and not a wrapped-up, solid, authoritative package of information we can rely on. So what teachers talk about is authority and the social relations among their students and between students and Wikipedia editors. I turn to these discussions now.

Cathlena Martin and Lisa Dusenberry believe a useful question to ask of any wiki pedagogy is this: Is it truly collaborative?

(206). The advantage of asking this question is that a record of what happened in a group appears as history on the wiki, and there is an option to open the audience to a larger public. As an example Dusenberry describes a classroom group she made responsible for specific grammar issues. The wiki showed how students had divided up the tasks and could constantly refer to the work of other group members. They created a tab, on their own initiative, for "group notes." Their individual responsibility and their dialectic with other group members and the group as a whole (represented by the group notes) reflects both the reality and accountability of the work done and a more thorough collaboration than is usually the default with students in groups who divide up the work, work independently, and sometimes fail to complete a task and then are "covered" by another member of the group. The other important aspect is the teacher "administrator" who has ultimate control by his or her ability to monitor the group and veto inappropriate action. For instance, Martin insisted that a group remove the phrase "Georgia Sucks" from the front page of its wiki, as it insulted an opposing football team (208–09).

In "Wikis as Collaborative Writing Tools," Susan Loudermilk Garza and Tommy Hern say that wikis provide the best possible environment for teaching writers how to deal constructively with conflict, because negotiation is hard-wired into the technology at the beginning of the writing process. In essence, conflict is built into the process early in the collaborative experience, because wiki authors must agree on procedures first, thus working through procedural conflict: How are we going to set this up? What are we going to call it? Who is going to do what? And so on. They must learn to work together as a team early in the process, negotiating or averting affective conflict. In this way, they can quickly move on to what Rebecca Burnett, Christianna I. White, and Ann Hill Duin call the "content, context, and concepts" of productive substantive conflict (151).

Garza and Hern's piece on conflict is published in the section of their article titled "Wiki and Composition Theory," which cites Donald Murray, Kenneth Bruffee, and John Trimbur ("Composition"), stating that their own work is an extension of Trimbur's piece with a different (not Marxist) focus.[46] According to Garza and Hern, Trimbur's piece focuses on the means of production and theirs on the means of producing a text. They say, "[W]e view collaboration . . . as being one of the 'delivery systems through which writing circulates.' . . . Instead of the program leading the process, the writer leads the program and develops the process."

Another significant piece of scholarship on wikis that explicitly uses the scholarship of Bruffee is Joe Moxley and Ryan Meehan's Web document "Collaboration, Literacy, Authorship: Using Social Networking Tools to Engage the Wisdom of Teachers." They link the importance of collaborative learning to Bruffee's work, the significance of social networking tools, and the importance of dissensus. Furthermore, they describe their wiki-based curriculum, involving ninety-eight teachers at the University of Southern Florida, with cautionary tales of collaboration, such as the importance of dissensus.

Matt Barton is perhaps the most influential scholar in the literature of the wiki, reflecting the passionate democratic aspirations of its practitioners. He draws directly on Bruffee, Trimbur, and Jürgen Habermas to link the possibilities of the wiki to earlier social-constructionist arguments and to a sense of citizenship, which he conceives as speaking truth to power. In "Embrace the Wiki Way," Barton celebrates the playfulness of the wiki and its transgressive nature. He argues against a concern with safety/privacy issues, making a political statement about the importance of setting up no safeguards in a wiki. A couple of playful examples are followed by this statement: "In short, wikis are protected not by code, or by law, but rather by the participation of an active wiki community" (contrasting police and neighbors). Barton lists some bad ideas for wiki use, including novels, portfolios, and argument papers—and gives reasons. He then offers a list of good ways to use wikis in classrooms that includes reference tools, bibliographies, class letters, handbooks, textbooks, and "[a]ny other project that does not require specified authorship or protected documents," noting that "[w]ikis are authored by communities, not individuals" ("Embrace").

Barton sees political potential in wiki pedagogy and believes in the theory-practice dialectic. In "The Future of Rational-Critical Debate," he outlines a theoretical framework for wikis that uses Habermas's notion of the public sphere. He compares Habermas's criteria for the functioning of a rational, equitable public sphere with the contemporary functioning of blogs, bulletin boards, and wikis.[47] As Habermas notes, the public sphere of the eighteenth century was based on the notion that the government could be questioned, that the debates were on issues that hadn't been debated before (creating new knowledge, rather than parroting or rehashing the old), and that everyone had an equal say (179). Privately owned media changed the terms by hierarchizing who could have the megaphone and who couldn't. News journals became lackeys because they were under the thumb of their employers. The free press became privately owned (179). Barton sees the same possibilities in electronic social devices and fears the same eclipsed public debate.

Although Barton embraces the egalitarian possibilities of the wiki, in using Habermas he seems unaware of the structural oppression that is possible in Habermas's model. Habermas's ideal, much like Bruffee's, assumes equal conversational partners, not taking into account the unequal material conditions and uneven cultural capital that complicate power relations within the group, giving some participants bigger voices than others. Barton has argued that wikis share Habermas's ideal of democratic interaction. They are within the lay public's capabilities to learn; they offer a ground for public debate; and they are open to all (182). One of the less obvious things that make wikis special (not easily commercialized) is the page history, which changes the commercialized "product" notion of writing into a human "process" notion of writing. Wikis document the social process of writing with revisions by individuals who collectively have written the document.

Barton's work in this text displays the utopian hope indulged in by wiki proponents, and networked classroom proponents before them. Vetter's review of wiki scholarship notes that more recent wiki scholars, such as Janice Fernheimer and Rebecca Lundin Wilson, have not necessarily seen democratic collaboration in their students' interactions with one another in wikis. Vetter concludes, in line with Bruffee and Dewey, that wiki pedagogy must be structured to encourage democratic participation. Using Stephen Thorne's "culture of use" concept, Vetter concludes that material conditions in relation to social culture are more important to a realization of true collaboration than is dependence on a particular technology ("Teaching" 15–17).

The apparent "failure" of collaborative, democratic principles can also function as an educational window into how things work. As I have discussed in earlier chapters, teachers' attention to the historical and material conditions of these technologies can enable students to examine these structures of power. For instance, flaming in synchronous discussions can provoke a discussion about structural racism (Faigley). Challenges to Wikipedia's authority can be discussed as public negotiations of what counts as knowledge and its threat to academic and financial structures. This critical understanding can be the fruition of the democratic potential of these technologies.

CONCLUSION

In this chapter, I have demonstrated the intermittent rise and fall of egalitarian hope in versions of collaborative learning afforded by various digital technologies. At the same time I have shown that early networked computer pedagogy was influenced by Dewey's pragmatism in that it was grounded in Bruffee's work and that influence continues in wiki pedagogy. That advocates of collaborative learning are initially inspired by utopian democratic visions does not seem to be a problem to me. Without the pursuit of ideals played out in practice, progressive teachers might not know what to aspire to. What does concern me is the recurrent dropping of history that I've documented in this chapter and in this book. When we know our history, we are able to reach back to our colleagues in other historical eras with different material conditions and ideological constraints and join with them, rather than assume that we're inventing something new. Commitment to educational and cultural reform is a longitudinal activism, and we can't afford to lose any allies.

8

A Reflective Conclusion

> We are alive
> Oh, and though we lie alone here in the dark
> Our souls will rise to carry the fire and light the spark
> To fight shoulder to shoulder and heart to heart.
> —Bruce Springsteen, "We Are Alive,"
> from *Wrecking Ball* (2012)

MY HISTORICAL SCAN IN THIS BOOK HAS REVEALED a rich diversity of practices. Most revealing are the ways in which collaborative learning has participated in the prevailing ideology of its political eras. Marxist scholar Greg Myers once told me as he was writing "Reality, Consensus, and Reform" that this participation is predictable, not subversive, and therefore not particularly interesting. But I disagree. Most of us who have written about our collaborative practices over the past eighty years have believed that we were doing something important, if in a small way, to support democratic practices. Cynthia Selfe might call it "a small potent gesture." The differences I have pointed out between collaborative practices in the 1930s and those in the 1950s, for instance, indicating the seeking of social justice on the one hand, and practices of surveillance on the other, show not only that we might be sometimes unaware of the implicit lessons reflected in our pedagogy, but also that, without knowing our history, we deprive ourselves of the possibility of benefiting from our historical allies, as I pointed out at the end of the last chapter. Collaborative learning in the past ninety years has been "discovered" at least six times, twice since I started the research that culminated in this book.

Here are some motives teachers have published to rationalize collaborative pedagogy, nearly all related to or resistant to John Dewey's motive of social reform. They range from social efficiency in the 1920s to social and economic survival in the 1930s. In the 1940s and 1950s, rationales start with detecting propaganda and end with saving labor. In the 1970s they include civil rights, avant-garde art, and support for writers. Knowledge construction and ideological awareness of class, race, and gender inform the thinking of the 1980s and 1990s, with computer-networked egalitarianism appearing near the end of the 1990s. In the 2000s, I see a second rise of knowledge construction in the wiki, the move from "community" to "alliance" in feminist pedagogy, and distributed work in professional writing.

As a writing program administrator, when I visit the classes of TAs I see mixed messages in some of their pedagogy. Some teachers put their students in groups, but then they participate, moving from group to group. Do they see themselves as monitors? As equals? When distinguished linguist James Sledd observed my class at the University of Texas in 1984, he sat silently in a group for the whole class, a paralyzing presence for the students, I'm sure, with his tall, white-coated, curmudgeonly Southern-gentleman presence, a stern expression on his face framed by white hair and black glasses.[48] When he reported on my class he wrote, "I don't see why she doesn't just teach." I thought that was a good question. That's a question I need to be able to answer.

Looking at possibilities for collaborative learning in the future, I suspect it will respond—as does rhetoric itself—to the unstable material and political conditions that open spaces for creative thought and democratic action. Three circumstances I'm interested in at the moment are the global network, the increasing currency of posthuman theory, and the new civil rights movements represented by Black Lives Matter and the disability rights organization ADAPT, among others. I'll address these interests briefly, framing them with two questions:

What vision of democracy is suitable for our era?

What are its consequences?

The first question is one articulated by Leonard J. Waks in "John Dewey and the Challenge of Progressive Education" (2013): "What vision of democracy is suitable for the global network era?" he asks (80). Is Dewey's ideal of democracy outdated? If so, what should replace it? And what are the consequences for education of each vision?

The second question is a modification of Waks's question: "What vision of democracy is suitable" for a world that involves objects and ideas on an equal and indivisible ground with human bodies? Laura Micciche notes that writers acknowledge dogs and notebooks, houses and coffee shops, as well as human partners and friends. Donna Phillips and Mindy Larson invite classroom paraphernalia into their frame, such as chalk, computers, and desks. What happens if we open our aperture to see objects around us as subjects themselves? Karen Barad's word is *entanglement*. What are the consequences of ignoring or embracing this perspective in our teaching? How does this affect the idea of collaborative learning?[49]

The third and most important question for me now is: "What vision of democracy is suitable" for an era of unfinished democracy, protest, and violence? Will our curricula change to meet the activist goals of Black Lives Matter and other prodemocracy advocates? What role might collaborative learning play in this? And what could be the consequences of any action we take?

I end this book, then, with curiosity, what my friend Linda Scott calls "curiosity at the edge of the unknown."[50]

NOTES

1. I have limited the scope of my investigation to the twentieth-century practices influenced by philosophical pragmatism, although it is clear that collaboration in educational practice has taken place well beyond these boundaries. One example is Lauren Fitzgerald's "'Torah Is Not Learned but in a Group': Talmud Study and Collaborative Learning." Another is Anne Gere's *Writing Groups: History, Theory, and Implications.*
2. The scope of this book is primarily limited to postsecondary teaching. Cooperative learning, largely practiced in K–12, is designed for students to work interdependently to accomplish closed-ended tasks, and is focused on knowledge acquisition. See Roger Johnson and David Johnson's cooperative learning website at www.co-operation.org/. Another form of collaboration that falls beyond the scope of this project is coauthoring. Lisa Ede and Andrea Lunsford have done the most significant and influential work on this subject.
3. *English Journal,* the precursor of *College English,* began in 1912, one year after the organization of the National Council of Teachers of English. In 1928, *English Journal* published a college edition, which lasted until 1939, when the college edition became *College English.*
4. See Russell 186–87 and Newkirk 204–5 for analyses of Dewey's stance on the role of the teacher.
5. For more about the Dalton Plan and the Project Method, see Holt, "Dewey and the 'Cult of Efficiency.'"
6. Rugg's series is titled *Man and His Changing Society* (Kliebard 204). The impact of the social reconstructionists is chronicled in the controversial journal *Social Frontier.*
7. Even among those who put students in groups with the goal of "socializing" their classrooms were teachers who practiced current-traditional rhetoric. For example, Berlin describes Ward's course as "a current-traditional approach to writing instruction emphasizing

arrangement and superficial correctness" but emphasizing the "social arts" as well in its inclusion of extemporaneous speeches and its structured student exchange (*Rhetoric and Reality* 82). As Karen Burke LeFevre has said, "A theorist may have a foot in both camps . . . [and a] teacher who adds a few group activities to the composition classroom does not automatically have a dialectical view of invention" (49).

8. My use of "expressive" and "social" rhetorics is in line with Berlin's "expressionistic" and "social-epistemic" rhetorics in his "Rhetoric and Ideology in the Writing Class." From Berlin's perspective, expressive rhetorics assume that knowledge lies within individuals. Social rhetorics assume that knowledge is created through the interaction of individuals in their material and social circumstances. Sherrie Gradin's "social expressivism" is a successful attempt to merge the two, to embrace the gray area between the two Berlin distinguished.

9. This problem still plagues collaborative pedagogy. For examples of critics of Kenneth Bruffee's collaborative learning who are concerned about the role of the individual in his model, see Johnson, Beade, and Stewart. For explanations of Bruffee's position, see his "Kenneth A. Bruffee Responds," his "Liberal Education," and Trimbur's "Consensus and Difference."

10. The Progressive Education Association was organized in 1919 as an association of teachers and parents who wanted to focus on the educational needs of individual students. Its membership peaked during the 1930s (with 7,400 members), when Dewey was its honorary president, and its focus broadened to include social and political issues. Its influence waned after World War II, and it disbanded in 1955.

11. *The Social Frontier: A Journal of Educational Criticism and Reconstruction* was published by the Progressive Education Association between 1934 and 1943.

12. Together *College English* and *College Composition and Communication* published thirty-one articles on collaborative pedagogy during the 1930s and eleven articles during the 1950s.

13. The authoritarian spell that Adolf Hitler wove over the German populace confused "groupthink" with the social construction of ideas. The conformity that charismatic figures compel is based on an individual, not a social, conception of knowledge. And the authority in the charismatic model is vertical, not horizontal. The "social relations" involved in collaborative learning take place among

the individuals in the group, not between each individual and the charismatic leader. It is the free play of ideas among peers that characterizes collaborative learning, not charismatic "groupthink," and not an abstract notion of democracy imposed upon a people.

14. See Squire.

15. In the statement, the US Office of Education (which later became the Department of Education) prioritized English as a subject "basic" to all other subjects and prioritized writing instruction over literature. It pledged to sponsor research and experimentation in the field and to initiate centers for the development and dissemination of this research (United States).

16. For the following description of Rogers's theory I am particularly indebted to Hall and Lindzey.

17. Rogerian therapy broadened the definition of "qualified therapist." In comparison to the years of training required to be a psychoanalyst or psychiatrist, client-centered therapy was promoted as requiring "little or no knowledge of personality diagnosis and dynamics in order to use it" (Hall and Lindzey 524).

18. The articles of Wolf, Margolis, Sara Winter, and Allan Wendt make up a group devoted to teaching in the context of psychotherapy. Margolis's and Winter's are responses to Wolf's piece. Margolis, a poetry therapist, supports Wolf's approach, but criticizes him for allowing his students' writing to remain anonymous. "We must help students share themselves as they are ready in biographical ways they can signature," notes Margolis (280). Winter, a psychologist and encounter-group leader who team-taught a course on male/female roles with Wolf, suggests that students may need more clear lines of authority than Wolf proposes (270) and that "relevance" may not be a realistic goal in light of the contemporary cultural diversity of college students (272). Wendt's article ("Who's a Yahoo!") describes his experiment teaching Swift within the framework of group therapy.

19. Stephen Nachmanovitch argues in *Free Play* that structure is often important for creativity. The chapter in which he argues this is called "The Power of Limits."

20. Sirc interweaves the art movement and the composition movement, reviving the principles of the Happening to reinvigorate composition. Some examples of art Happenings he describes thus:

- At the culmination of Allan Kaprow's *Spring Happening,* from Kaprow's performance notes: "car horn starts constant sound, lawn mower starts, pushed by tar paper figure, moves through all eight rooms [of the gallery] cutting swath through leaves blowing them all over" (qtd. in Sirc, *English* 131)

- One of George Brecht's "event-scores" had participants "[a]rrange to observe a sign indicating direction of travel. • travel in the indicated direction • travel in another direction" (qtd. in Sirc, *English* 29)

- Wolf Vostell's itinerary for his *Cityrama* had participants tour post-bomb Cologne and "stand on the corner [of Luebecker Street and Maybach Street] for about five minutes and ponder whether six or thirty-six human beings perished during the night of the thousand-bomber air raid" (qtd. in Sirc, *English* 124)

21. For an article devoted to the topic of evaluating collaborative pedagogy, see Harvey Wiener's "Collaborative Learning in the Classroom: A Guide to Evaluation." Wiener suggests that collaborative learning demands a concept of evaluation appropriate to its nature. For a discussion of research in collaborative practice, see Trimbur's "Collaborative Learning and Teaching Writing" 106–9.

22. This is not the case with the Happening, says Bruffee, because although students may become involved in it, "they are not responsible for it, or for each other's learning during or after it" ("The Way Out" 461).

23. Murray has had a much greater influence on innovative pedagogy than is reflected in my discussion here. I have not given Murray a key role in this study because his work is not primarily concerned with student groups, but instead with the conference method, in which the relationship between student and teacher is primary. One of his many pieces is his 1973 article with Lester A. Fisher in *College English*, "Perhaps the Professor Should Cut Class."

24. For an article on the Story Workshop written by the originator of the method, see John Schultz.

25. This description is based on a compilation of material from *Writing without Teachers* 76–145, *Writing with Power* 272 and 276, and *Embracing Contraries* 258–59 and 274.

26. The excellent work of Jacqueline Jones Royster, Krista Ratcliffe, and Joyce Irene Middleton is significant in this context in that they address the importance of listening in the framework of white privilege. (*White supremacy* is a more accurate term, in my opinion.)

27. Elbow was a FIPSE evaluator for Bruffee's 1981 Brooklyn College Summer Institute in Peer Tutor Training and Collaborative Learning, and a participant in the following summer's reconvening of the

1980 and 1981 participants. Elbow wrote his report of the 1981 institute in the form of a letter to Bruffee; Bruffee replied in kind. The exchange reflects an elucidating delineation of their different conceptions of the purpose of the group and the nature of authority in the classroom. John Trimbur discusses this exchange in "Paper Trails."

28. See also Paula Beck et al., "Training and Using Peer Tutors," and Bruffee's "Two Related Issues in Peer Tutoring: Program Structure and Tutor Training."

29. See Harvey Kail, Paula Gillespie, and Bradley Hughes's longitudinal study of the intellectual growth of peer tutors.

30. Bruffee's widely used textbook was first published in 1972 and went through five editions. His success with peer tutoring gained him a grant from the US Department of Education's Fund for the Improvement of Postsecondary Education (FIPSE) to fund a series of summer institutes that took place during the summers of 1980–83. The collaboration that took place during these institutes helped spawn peer-tutoring programs based on collaborative learning in colleges across the country, and a spinoff of the institute (also funded by FIPSE) was conducted by Carol Stanger for her colleagues in Connecticut. The influence of the collaboration prompted by Bruffee's institute is reflected in the work of other participants, such as Harvey Kail's "Collaborative Learning in Context: The Problem with Peer Tutoring" and John Trimbur's "Collaborative Learning and Teaching Writing."

31. For a fuller description of the peer practices of Elbow and Bruffee, see Holt, "The Value of Written Peer Criticism."

32. For a fascinating reading of the historical context of Bruffee's work, see Hawkes.

33. Elbow's work on nonstandard English, however, shows his subsequent thinking in this matter. See "Inviting the Mother Tongue" and *Vernacular Eloquence*. For a thorough critique of Elbow and Bruffee, as well as contact zone pedagogies, see Horner's *Terms of Work*.

34. Although Shor takes care not to intervene in student group discussions so long as they remain on-task, he makes a point of mentioning that he intervenes with groups that veer off-task into personal and sports talk. He writes that "[t]his is not a permissive pedagogy which allows students to do whatever they want with class time" (48). For a different perspective on student off-task discourse, see Brooke's article on the value of student underlife.

35. This perspective is characteristic of second-wave feminist pedagogy. More confrontational third-wave feminist pedagogy is represented by bell hooks and Allison Dorsey.

36. For debates on the issue of difference in feminism, see Waller and Marcos, specifically Marguerite Waller's "'One Voice Kills Both Our Voices'" and Shu-mei Shih, Sylvia Marcos, Obioma Nnaemeka, and Waller's "Conversation on 'Feminist Imperialism and the Politics of Difference.'"

37. For a pedagogical illustration of differences between second- and third-wave feminism, see my "Teaching US and Transnational Feminisms with *Thelma and Louise* (1991) and *Chaos* (2001)."

38. Dorsey identifies patterns of many white students' responses, which she calls the 4 D's—Discovery, Dismay, Denial, and Dismissal.

39. The International Writing Centers Association (IWCA) began as the National Writing Centers Association under the aegis of NCTE in 1983 as an outcropping of a regional association and with the initiative of Nancy McCracken. In 1997 it became independent from NCTE. For more history of the organization, see Joyce Kinkead's *Writing Center Journal* article "The National Writing Centers Association as Mooring: A Personal History of the First Decade."

40. "Usability research," which focuses on the audience as stakeholder, was developed by Stuart Blythe.

41. Selfe sees new media as digital (*Writing New Media* 43). Wysocki et al. see new media as any text that in its production calls attention to its own materiality (15). According to Ball, new media are multimodal and digital (as in Selfe's view) but with the addition that their rhetoric is not linear but multimodal.

42. As first introduced by the Daedalus Group's InterChange and then later with MOOs, or educational chat spaces. In 1990, another vehicle was invented for gaming purposes by Stephen White at Princeton University and then adapted for educational purposes in many universities. MOOs offered a non-Web-based environment for both synchronous conferences and for the composition of extended spaces and gamelike "avatars" based on textual description. Early MOOs were completely text-based, while later MOOs became more graphic, with a commonly used Web interface, enCore Xpress, which splits the screen into two spaces. The left side is the traditional text-only descriptions of the "space" or "room" your player is in; the right side is the weblike graphical version where images and links can be placed. The similarity of MOO virtual reality to gaming environments potentially yields more playful, creative,

and intrinsically motivated activities and learning. MOOs can be ideal spaces for small-group collaborative projects in which groups create rooms (or other spaces) that feature objects, robot characters, and documents, images, and links. The idea is to represent knowledge about a topic (say, Plato's rhetoric in "The Phaedrus," or the impact of the railroad on relations between American Indians and whites in the US West) as something a reader can at least partly experience. Work groups can meet in the MOO and jointly discuss and work on projects, saving discussion transcripts if need be.

43. See Kemp for a discussion of the history of Daedalus.

44. For an excellent source that offers strategies for organizing wikis and other digital environments (including blogs and social media) in a collaborative digital classroom, see Tekobbe, Lazcano-Pry, and Roen.

45. Cummings offers a history of the wiki, a technology pioneered by Ward Cunningham, a moderator of an email list of software developers in 1995. Cunningham created a feature to acquaint members with the history of comments on a particular subject to avoid needless repetition (5). In 2000, Jimmy Wales created Nupedia, an online version of a traditional encyclopedia with peer-reviewed scholarly entries. In 2005, Wales changed Nupedia to Wikipedia, the open-source collaborative site that it largely is now (6).

46. It is hard, nevertheless, to understand how to exclude Marxism from Trimbur's article, which is a Marxist analysis of the circulation of writing.

47. Barton reminds us that password-protected wikis, perfect for composition classes, are not true wikis, not as valuable because they are not open to all ("Future" 183).

48. James Sledd lived an activist career at the University of Texas, and he would have been proud to be remembered as a curmudgeon. He wrote a glowing recommendation letter for a graduate student peer of mine, but referred to the student by his nickname, "Snake," throughout the letter. His intellect and humor and honesty were characteristic of his significant and persuasive work on the CCCC *Statement on Students' Right to Their Own Language.* I invite you to read Beth Daniell's article "James Sledd: In Memoriam," published in 2003.

49. The wisdom of deciding a truth by its consequences was proffered by William James in his lecture "What Pragmatism Means."

50. When I first wrote this sentence, it was meant to be the last sentence of the book. Now it is the first week of Donald Trump's presidency.

Iraqi refugees who were in midair when he signed an executive order stopping travelers from six predominantly Muslim countries from entering the United States are being detained at airports. Last week Kellyanne Conway introduced and defended the notion of "alternative facts." And theoretical imaginings about the possibilities of collaborative learning give way in my mind to a hard look at collective action, and its possibilities.

WORKS CITED

Abercrombie, M.L.J. *The Anatomy of Judgment: An Investigation into the Processes of Perception and Reasoning.* London: Hutchinson, 1960. Print.

Applebee, Arthur N. *Tradition and Reform in the Teaching of English: A History.* Urbana: NCTE, 1974. Print.

"Athens Lunatic Asylum." *Wikipedia: The Free Encyclopedia.* Wikimedia Foundation. 30 June 2013. Web. 23 Aug. 2013.

Babin, Edith, and Kimberly Harrison. *Contemporary Composition Studies: A Guide to Theorists and Terms.* Westport: Greenwood, 1999. *EBSCOhost.* Web. 1 May 2017.

Barad, Karen. *Meeting the Universe Halfway: Quantum Physics and the Entanglement of Matter and Meeting.* Duke UP, 2007. Print.

Barnes, Walter. "American Youth and Their Language." *English Journal* 26.4 (1937): 283–90. Print.

Barton, Matt[hew D.]. "Embrace the Wiki Way (Reprint)." *Mattchat.us.* 1 Nov. 2013. Web. 2 May 2017.

———. "The Future of Rational-Critical Debate in Online Public Spheres. " *Computers and Composition* 22 (2005): 177–90. Print.

Bawarshi, Anis, and Stephanie Pelkowski. "Postcolonialism and the Idea of a Writing Center." *Writing Center Journal* 19.2 (1999): 41–58. Print.

Beade, Pedro. "Comment and Response: More Comments on 'Social Construction, Language, and the Authority of Knowledge: A Bibliographical Essay.'" *College English* 49.6 (1987): 707–08. Print.

Beck, Paula, Thom Hawkins, Marcia Silver, Kenneth A. Bruffee, Judy Fishman, and Judith T. Matsunobu. "Training and Using Peer Tutors." *College English* 40.4 (1978): 432–49. Print.

Benjamin, Edwin B. "Group Dynamics in Freshman English." *College English* 19.3 (1957): 122–23. Print.

Bennis, Warren G., and Herbert A. Shepard. "A Theory of Group Development." *Human Relations* 9.4 (1956): 415–37. Print.

Bentman, Raymond. "Reconsideration: Student-Directed Courses." *College English* 34.3 (1972): 461–64. Print.

Berlin, James A. "Rhetoric and Ideology in the Writing Class." *College English* 50.5 (1988): 477–94. Print.

———. *Rhetoric and Reality: Writing Instruction in American Colleges, 1900–1985.* Carbondale: Southern Illinois UP, 1987. Print.

Berzsenyi, Christyne A. "Teaching Interlocutor Relationships in Electronic Classrooms." *Computers and Composition* 16.2 (1999): 229–46. Print.

Bestor, Arthur Eugene. *Educational Wastelands: The Retreat from Learning in Our Public Schools.* Urbana: U of Illinois P, 1953. Print.

Blair, Kristine. "Literacy, Dialogue, and Difference in the 'Electronic Contact Zone.'" *Computers and Composition* 15.3 (1998): 317–29. Print.

Blythe, Stuart. "Designing Online Courses: User-Centered Practices." *Computers and Composition* 18.4 (2001): 329–46. Print.

Boquet, Elizabeth H. "'Our Little Secret': A History of Writing Centers, Pre– to Post–Open Admissions." *College Composition and Communication* 50.3 (1999): 463–82. Print.

Borczon, John A. "Learning and Transformation: How Students and Teachers Define and Shape Each Other in the Classroom and in Pedagogic Literature." Diss. Ohio U, 2010. Print.

Bräuer, Gerd. "Extending Writing Center Work toward the Community: Writing and Reading Support for Asylum Seekers in the City of Leipzig." Athens International Writing Centers Conference. Hellenic American U, Athens. 9–10 Nov. 2007. Address.

Briggs, Harold E. "Applications of the Principles of Group Dynamics in the College Classroom." *College English* 12.2 (1950): 84–90. Print.

Brooke, Robert. "Underlife and Writing Instruction." *College Composition and Communication* 38.2 (1987): 141–53. Print.

Bruffee, Kenneth A. "The Brooklyn Plan: Attaining Intellectual Growth through Peer-Group Tutoring." *Liberal Education* 64.4 (1978): 447–68. Print.

———. "Collaborative Learning: Some Practical Models." *College English* 34.5 (1973): 634–43. Print.

———. "Collaborative Learning and the 'Conversation of Mankind.'" *College English* 46.7 (1984): 635–52. Print.

———. "Kenneth A. Bruffee Responds." *College English* 48.1 (1986): 77–78. Print.

———. Letter to Peter Elbow discussing his "Report on Summer Institute, 1981." 1981. MS. National Archive of Composition and Rhetoric. U of New Hampshire Lib., Durham.

———. "Liberal Education and the Social Justification of Belief." *Liberal Education* 68.2 (1982): 95–114. Print.

————. *A Short Course in Writing: Practical Rhetoric for Teaching Composition through Collaborative Learning.* 3rd ed. Boston: Little, 1985. Print.

————. "Two Related Issues in Peer Tutoring: Program Structure and Tutor Training." *College Composition and Communication* 31.1 (1980): 76–80. Print.

————. "The Way Out: A Critical Survey of Innovations in College Teaching, with Special Reference to the December, 1971, Issue of *College English.*" *College English* 33.4 (1972): 457–70. Print.

Burnett, Rebecca E., Christianna I. White, and Ann Hill Duin. "Locating Collaboration: Reflections, Features, and Influences." *Foundations for Teaching Technical Communication: Theory, Practice, and Program Design.* Ed. Katherine Staples and Cezar Ornatowski. Greenwich: Ablex, 1997. 133–60. Print.

Carroll, Elsie C. "Freshening Freshman English." *English Journal* College Ed. 20.9 (1931): 762–68. Print.

Chordas, Nina. "Classrooms, Pedagogies, and the Rhetoric of Equality." *College Composition and Communication* 43.2 (1992): 214–24. Print.

Clary-Lemon, Jennifer. "The Racialization of Composition Studies: Scholarly Rhetoric of Race since 1990." *College Composition and Communication* 61.2 (2009): W1–17. Print.

Coles, W. E., Jr. "The Sense of Nonsense as a Design for Sequential Writing Assignments." *College Composition and Communication* 21.1 (1970): 27–34. Print.

Cooper, Marilyn. "Postmodern Possibilities in Electronic Conversations." *Passions, Pedagogies, and Twenty-First Century Technologies.* Ed. Gail E. Hawisher and Cynthia L. Selfe. Logan: Utah State UP; Urbana: NCTE, 1999. 140–60. Print.

Cremin, Lawrence A. *The Transformation of the School: Progressivism in American Education, 1876–1957.* New York: Vintage, 1961. Print.

Cummings, Robert E. "What Was a Wiki, and Why Do I Care? A Short and Usable History of Wikis." Cummings and Barton 1–17.

Cummings, Robert E., and Matt Barton. *Wiki Writing: Collaborative Learning in the College Classroom.* Ann Arbor: U of Michigan P, 2008. Print.

Daedalus Group. "Educational Software and Services for Collaborative Learning and the Writing Process." Daedalus Group, n.d. Web. 12 Aug. 2013.

Daniell, Beth. "In Memoriam: James Sledd." *College Composition and Communication* 55.2 (2003): 217–20. Print.

Deemer, Charles. "English Composition as a Happening." *College English* 29.2 (1967): 121–26. Print.

Denny, Harry C. *Facing the Center: Toward an Identity Politics of One-to-One Mentoring.* Logan: Utah State UP, 2010. Print.

Dewey, John. *Democracy and Education: An Introduction to the Philosophy of Education.* New York: Macmillan, 1916. Print.

———. *Experience and Education.* New York: Macmillan, 1938. Print.

———. *Human Nature and Conduct: An Introduction to Social Psychology.* New York: Holt, 1922. Print.

———. "Individuality and Experience." *Journal of the Barnes Foundation* 2 (1930): 1–6. Print.

———. "President Hutchins' Proposals to Remake Higher Education." *Social Frontier* 3.22 (1937): 103–04. Rpt. in *The Social Frontier: A Critical Reader.* Ed. Eugene F. Provenzo. New York: Lang, 2011. 198–202. Print.

———. *The School and Society.* 2nd rev. ed. Chicago: U of Chicago P, 1916. Print.

Diffenbaugh, G. L. "Communal Outlining." *English Journal* 19.9 (1930): 744–47. Print.

DiMatteo, Anthony. "Under Erasure: A Theory for Interactive Writing in Real Time." *Computers and Composition* 7 (1990): 71–84. Web. 2 May 2017.

Donahue, Christiane. "'Internationalization' and Composition Studies: Reorienting the Discourse." *College Composition and Communication* 61.2 (2009): 212–43. Print.

Dorsey, Allison. "'white girls' and 'Strong Black Women': Reflections on a Decade of Teaching Black History at Predominantly White Institutions (PWIs)." Macdonald and Sánchez-Casal 203–32.

Ede, Lisa, and Andrea Lunsford. "Why Write . . . Together?" *Rhetoric Review* 1.2 (1983): 150–57. Print.

Educator's Washington Dispatch. *Two Lessons in Group Dynamics: So You Appointed a Committee; When You Run a Conference.* Washington, DC: Educator's Washington Dispatch, 1948. Print.

Ehrenreich, Barbara. *Fear of Falling: The Inner Life of the Middle Class.* New York: Harper, 1990. Print.

Elbow, Peter. "Closing My Eyes as I Speak: An Argument for Ignoring Audience." *College English* 49.1 (1987): 50–69. Print.

———. "Comment on Ken Bruffee." *College English* 34.3 (1972): 466. Print.

———. "The Definition of Teaching." *College English* 30.3 (1968): 187–201. Print.

———. *Embracing Contraries: Explorations in Learning and Teaching.* New York: Oxford UP, 1986. Print.

———. "Exploring My Teaching." *College English* 32.7 (1971): 743–53. Print.

———. "Inviting the Mother Tongue: Beyond 'Mistakes,' 'Bad English,' and 'Wrong Language.'" *JAC* 19.3 (1999): 359–88. Web. 13 May 2017.

———. "A Method for Teaching Writing." *College English* 30.2 (1968): 115–25. Print.

———. *Vernacular Eloquence: What Speech Can Bring to Writing.* New York: Oxford UP, 2012. Print.

———. *Writing with Power: Techniques for Mastering the Writing Process.* New York: Oxford UP, 1981. Print.

———. *Writing without Teachers.* New York: Oxford UP, 1973. Print.

Elbow, Peter, and Pat Belanoff. *A Community of Writers: A Workshop Course in Writing.* New York: Random, 1989. Print.

Elliott, Una B., and George Adrian Kuyper. "Remedial Reading—Group Treatment." *College English* 2.1 (1940): 58–62. Print.

Faigley, Lester. *Fragments of Rationality: Postmodernity and the Subject of Composition.* Pittsburgh: U of Pittsburgh P, 1992. Print.

Fisher, Lester A., and Donald M. Murray. "Perhaps the Professor Should Cut Class." *College English* 35.2 (1973): 169–73. Print.

Fitzgerald, Lauren. "'Torah Is Not Learned but in a Group': Collaborative Learning and Talmud Study." *Judaic Perspectives in Rhetoric and Composition Studies.* Ed. Deborah Holdstein and Andrea Greenbaum. Cresskill: Hampton, 2008. 23–42. Print.

Fox, Catherine. "The Race to Truth: Disarticulating Critical Thinking from Whiteness." *Pedagogy* 2.2 (2002): 197–212. Print.

Franco, Miguel. "A/Void [in] Open Admissions: Decolonizing College Composition. 2016. MS.

Freire, Paulo. *Pedagogy of the Oppressed.* Trans. Myra Bergman Ramos. 30th ed. New York: Continuum, 2000. Print.

Freire, Paulo, and Ana Maria Araújo Freire. *Pedagogy of Hope: Reliving Pedagogy of the Oppressed.* London: Continuum, 2004. Print.

Garza, Susan Loudermilk, and Tommy Hern. "Using Wikis as Collaborative Writing Tools: Something Wiki this Way Comes—or Not!" *Kairos* 10.1 (2005): n pag. Web. 23 Aug. 2013.

George, E. Laurie. "Taking Women Professors Seriously: Female Authority in the Computerized Classroom." *Computers and Composition* 7 (1990): 45–52. Web. 2 May 2017.

Gere, Anne Ruggles. *Writing Groups: History, Theory, and Implications.* Carbondale: Southern Illinois UP, 1987. Print.

Gibson, Walker. "Freshman English in Sections of 150." *College English* 22.7 (1961): 501–03. Print.

Gitterman, Alex. "Collaborative Learning and Teaching." *Writing Center Journal* 28.2 (2008): 60–71. Print.

Gradin, Sherrie L. *Romancing Rhetorics: Social Expressivist Perspectives on the Teaching of Writing.* Portsmouth: Heinemann, 1995. Print.

Graff, Gerald. *Professing Literature: An Institutional History.* Chicago: U of Chicago P, 1987. Print.

Hall, Calvin S. and Gardner Lindzey. *Theories of Personality.* 2nd ed. New York: Wiley, 1970. Print.

Harasim, Linda M. *Learning Theory and Online Technology: How New Technologies Are Transforming Learning Opportunities.* New York: Routledge, 2012. Print.

Harold, Brent. "Beyond Student-Centered Teaching: The Dialectical Materialist Form of a Literature Course." *College English* 34.2 (1972): 200–12. Print.

Harris, Joseph. "After Dartmouth: Growth and Conflict in English." *College English* 53.6 (1991): 631–46. Print.

Hatfield, W. Wilbur. "Social Changes and 'English.'" *English Journal* 22.7 (1933): 536–41. Print.

Hawkes, Peter. "Vietnam Protests, Open Admissions, Peer Tutor Training, and the Brooklyn Institute: Tracing Kenneth Bruffee's Collaborative Learning." *Writing Center Journal* 28.2 (2008): 25–32. Print.

Hawkins, Thom. "Group Inquiry Techniques for Teaching Writing." *College English* 37.7 (1976): 637–46. Print.

Hayakawa, S. I. "Learning to Think and to Write: Semantics in Freshman English." *College Composition and Communication* 13.1 (1962): 5–8. Print.

Herman, George. "The 'Oregon Plan.'" *College English* 22.4 (1961): 284. Print.

Hertz-Lazarowitz, Rachel. "Cooperative Learning in Israel's Jewish and Arab Schools: A Community Approach." *Theory into Practice* 38.2 (1999): 105–13. Print.

Holcomb, Christopher. "A Class of Clowns: Spontaneous Joking in Computer-Assisted Discussions." *Computers and Composition* 14.1 (1997): 3–18. Print.

Holt, Mara. "Dewey and the 'Cult of Efficiency': Competing Ideologies in Collaborative Pedagogies of the 1920s." *Journal of Advanced Composition* 14.1 (1994): 73–92. Web. 8 Aug. 2017.

———. "The Importance of Dissent to Collaborative Learning." *Writing Center Journal* 28.2 (2008): 52–59. Print.

———. "Teaching US and Transnational Feminisms with *Thelma and Louise* (1991) and *Chaos* (2001)." *The International Journal of the Arts in Society: Annual Review* 4.6 (2010): 41–52. Print.

———. "The Value of Written Peer Criticism." *College Composition and Communication* 43.3 (1992): 384–92. Print.

Hood, Carra Leah. "Editing Out Obscenity: *Wikipedia* and Writing Pedagogy." *Computers and Composition Online* (Theory into Practice Section, Spring 2009): n. pag. Web. 2 May 2017.

Horner, Bruce. *Terms of Work for Composition*. NY: SUNY Press, 2000. Print.

Horner, Bruce, and John Trimbur. "English Only and US College Composition." *College Composition and Communication* 53.4 (2002): 594–630. Print.

Hunter, Susan. "A Woman's Place *Is* in the Composition Classroom: Pedagogy, Gender, and Difference." *Rhetoric Review* 9.2 (1991): 230–45. Print.

Hutchins, Robert M. *The Higher Learning in America*. New Haven: Yale UP, 1936. Print.

International Writing Centers Association. Home page. *Writingcenters.org*. International Writing Centers Association, n.d. Web. 28 May 2012.

Irlen, Harvey Stuart. "Toward Confronting Freshmen." *College Composition and Communication* 21.1 (1970): 35–40. Print.

James, William. "What Pragmatism Means." *Writings, 1902–1910*. Ed. Bruce Kucklick. New York: Lib. of America, 1987. 505–22.

Jarratt, Susan C. "Feminism and Composition: The Case for Conflict." *Contending with Words: Composition and Rhetoric in a Postmodern Age*. Ed. Patricia Harkin and John Schilb. New York: MLA, 1991. Print.

Johnson, Thomas S. "A Comment on 'Collaborative Learning and the "Conversation of Mankind.'"" *College English* 48.1 (1986): 76. Print.

Jones, Edith. "Teaching Conversation." *English Journal* 20.3 (1931): 210–19. Print.

Jones, Granville H. "Post Mortem: Student-Directed Courses I and II." *College English* 33.3 (1971): 284–93. Print.

Kail, Harvey. "Collaborative Learning in Context: The Problem with Peer Tutoring." *College English* 45.6 (1983): 594–99. Print.

———. "Innovation and Repetition: The Brooklyn College Summer Institute in Training Peer Writing Tutors Twenty-five Years Later." *Writing Center Journal* 28.2 (2008): 43–51. Print.

————, ed. *Kenneth Bruffee.* Spec. issue of *Writing Center Journal* 28.2 (2008): 3–97. Print.

Kail, Harvey, Paula Gillespie, and Bradley Hughes. *The Peer Writing Tutor Alumni Research Project.* U of Wisconsin–Madison, 2015. Web. 15 July 2015.

Kail, Harvey, and John Trimbur. "The Politics of Peer Tutoring." *WPA: Writing Program Administration* 11.1–2 (1987) 5–12. Print.

Kates, Susan. "Literacy, Voting Rights, and the Citizenship Schools in the South, 1957–1970." *College Composition and Communication* 57.3 (2006): 479–502. Print.

Kaye/Kantrowitz, Melanie. "Representation, Entitlement, and Voyeurism: Teaching across Difference." Macdonald and Sánchez-Casal 281–98.

Kelly, Lou. "Toward Competence and Creativity in an Open Class." *College English* 34.5 (1973): 644–60. Print.

Kemp, Fred. "The Origins of ENFI, Network Theory, and Computer-Based Collaborative Writing Instruction at the University of Texas." *Network-Based Classrooms: Promises and Realities.* Ed. Bertram C. Bruce, Joy Kreeft Peyton, and Trent Batson. Cambridge: Cambridge UP, 1993. 161–80. Print.

Kerr, Elizabeth M. "The Research Paper as a Class Enterprise." *College English* 13.4 (1952): 204–08. Print.

Kinkead, Joyce. "The National Writing Centers Association as Mooring: A Personal History of the First Decade." *Writing Center Journal* 16.2 (1996): 131–43. Print.

Kliebard, Herbert M. *The Struggle for the American Curriculum, 1893–1958.* New York: Routledge, 1987. Print.

Kolko, Beth E. "Cultural Studies in/and the Networked Writing Classroom." *The Online Writing Classroom.* Ed. Susanmarie Harrington, Rebecca Rickly, and Michael Day. Cresskill: Hampton, 2000. 29–43. Print.

Laird, Charlton. "Freshman English during the Flood." *College English* 18.3 (1956): 131–38. Print.

Lathan, Rhea Estelle. *Freedom Writing: African American Civil Rights Literacy Activism, 1955–1967.* Urbana: CCCC/NCTE, 2015. Print.

LeFevre, Karen Burke. *Invention as a Social Act.* Carbondale: Southern Illinois UP, 1986. Print.

Leitch, Vincent B. *American Literary Criticism from the Thirties to the Eighties.* New York: Columbia UP, 1988. Print.

Lerner, Neal. *The Idea of a Writing Laboratory.* Carbondale: Southern Illinois UP, 2009. Print.

Lu, Min-Zhan, and Bruce Horner. "The Problematic of Experience: Re-defining Critical Work in Ethnography and Pedagogy." *College English* 60.3 (1998): 257–77. Print.

Luchte, Jeanne. "Computer Programs in the Writing Center: A Bibliographical Essay." *Writing Center Journal* 8.1 (1987): 11–19. Print.

Lunsford, Andrea A., and Lisa Ede. *Writing Together: Collaboration in Theory and Practice.* N.p.: Bedford-St. Martin's, 2011. Print.

Lutz, William D. "Making Freshman English a Happening." *College Composition and Communication* 22.1 (1971): 35–38. Print.

Lyman, R. L. "Normalizing English Instruction." *English Journal* 21.2 (1932): 89–96. Print.

Lynn, Marvin. "Inserting the 'Race' into Critical Pedagogy: An Analysis of 'Race-Based Epistemologies.'" *Educational Philosophy and Theory* 36.2 (2004): 153–65.

Macdonald, Amie A., and Susan Sánchez-Casal, eds. *Twenty-First-Century Feminist Classrooms: Pedagogies of Identity and Difference.* New York: Palgrave, 2002. Print.

Macrorie, Ken. *Uptaught.* New York: Hayden, 1970. Print.

———. "To Be Read." *English Journal* 57.5 (1968): 686-692. Print.

Manchester, William. *The Glory and the Dream: A Narrative History of America, 1932–1972.* 2 vols. Boston: Little, 1974. Print.

Margolis, Gary. "Taking It All Off: Teaching in the Therapeutic Classroom." *College English* 33.3 (1971): 277–83. Print.

Martin, Cathlena, and Lisa Dusenberry. "Wiki Lore and Politics in the Classroom." Cummings and Barton 204–15.

Matsuda, Paul Kei. "The Myth of Linguistic Homogeneity in US College Composition." *College English* 68.6 (2006): 637–51. Print.

McKinney, Jackie Grutsch. "New Media Matters: Tutoring in the Late Age of Print." *Writing Center Journal* 29.2 (2009): 28–51. Print.

Micciche, Laura R. "Writing Material." *College English* 76.6 (2014): 488–505. Print.

Middleton, Joyce Irene. "Echoes from the Past: Learning How to Listen, Again." *The Sage Handbook of Rhetorical Studies.* Ed. Andrea A. Lunsford, Kirt H. Wilson, and Rosa A. Eberly. London: Sage, 2008. 353–71. Print.

———. "Rhetorical Listening: When the Eye Defers to the Ear for Civic Discourse." *English Journal* 101.1 (2011): 105–07. Print.

Mohanty, Chandra Talpade. *Feminism without Borders: Decolonizing Theory, Practicing Solidarity.* Durham: Duke UP, 2003. Print.

Moxley, Joe, and Ryan Meehan. "Collaboration, Literacy, Authorship: Using Social Networking Tools to Engage the Wisdom of Teachers." *Kairos* 12.1 (2007): n. pag. Web. 19 May 2017.

Murray, Donald M. "Finding Your Own Voice: Teaching Composition in an Age of Dissent." *College Composition and Communication* 20.2 (1969): 118–23. Print.

Murray, Donald M., and Irwin Hashimoto. "Mini-Symposium." Rev. of *Writing with Power: Techniques for Mastering the Writing Process,* by Peter Elbow. *College Composition and Communication* 33.2 (1982): 208–12. Print.

Murray, Marge T. "A Radical Pedagogy of Composition." *The Writing Instructor* 5 (1986): 85–95. Print.

Myers, Greg. "Greg Myers Responds." *College English* 49.2 (1987): 211–14. Print.

———. "Reality, Consensus, and Reform in the Rhetoric of Composition Teaching." *College English* 48.2 (1986): 154–74. Print.

Nachmanovitch, Stephen. *Free Play: Improvisation in Life and Art.* New York: Penguin, 1990.

Newkirk, Thomas. *More Than Stories: The Range of Children's Writing.* Portsmouth: Heinemann, 1989. Print.

Ohmann, Richard. "In Lieu of a New Rhetoric." *College English* 26.1 (1964): 17–22. Print.

Okawa, Gail Y., Thomas Fox, Lucy J. Y. Chang, Shayna R. Windsor, Frank Bella Chavez Jr., and LaGuan Hayes. "Multi-cultural Voices: Peer Tutoring and Critical Reflection in the Writing Center." *Writing Center Journal* 30.1 (2010): 40–65. Print.

Olson, Gary A. "Working with Difference: Critical Race Studies and the Teaching of Composition." *Composition Studies in the New Millennium: Rereading the Past, Rewriting the Future.* Ed. Lynn Z. Bloom, Donald A. Daiker, and Edward M. White. Carbondale: Southern Illinois UP, 2003. 208–21. Print.

Opdenacker, Liesbeth, and Luuk Van Waes. "Implementing an Open Process Approach to a Multilingual Online Writing Center: The Case of *Calliope.*" *Computers and Composition* 24.3 (2007): 247–65. Print.

O'Reilley, Mary Rose. *The Peaceable Classroom.* Portsmouth: Boynton, 1993.

Pace, Sara P. "Feminist Pedagogy and Daedalus Online." *Academic Exchange Quarterly* 6.1 (2002): 104–09. Print.

Parker, Laurence, and David O. Stovall. "Actions Following Words: Critical Race Theory Connects to Critical Pedagogy." *Educational Philosophy and Theory* 36.2 (2004): 167–82. Print.

Parkhurst, Helen. *Education on the Dalton Plan.* New York: Dutton, 1922. Print.

Parks, Stephen. *Class Politics: The Movement for the Students' Right to Their Own Language.* Urbana: NCTE, 2000. *ProQuest Ebook Central.* Web. 1 May 2017.

Phillips, Donna Kalmbach, and Mindy Legard Larson. "The Teacher-Student Writing Conference Reimaged: *entangled becoming-writingconferencing.*" *Gender and Education* 25.6 (2013): 722–37. Print.

Prendergast, Catherine. "Race: The Absent Presence in Composition Studies." *College Composition and Communication* 50.1 (1998): 36–53. Print.

Purdy, James P. "When the Tenets of Composition Go Public: A Study of Writing in Wikipedia." *College Composition and Communication* 61.2 (2009): 351–73. Print.

Racine, Sam, Denise Dilworth, and Lee-Ann M. Kastman Breuch. "Getting to Know Audiences in Cyberspace: A Usability Approach to Designing Skill Centers for Online Writing Centers." *The Journal of the Midwest Modern Language Association* 33.2 (2000): 58–78. Print.

Ratcliffe, Krista. *Rhetorical Listening: Identification, Gender, Whiteness.* Carbondale: Southern Illinois UP, 2005. Print.

———. "Rhetorical Listening: A Trope for Interpretive Invention and a 'Code of Cross-Cultural Conduct.'" *College Composition and Communication* 51.2 (1999): 195–224. Print.

Regan, Alison. "'Type Normal like the Rest of Us': Writing, Power and Homophobia in the Networked Composition Classroom." *Computers and Composition* 10.4 (1993): 11–23. Print.

Roberts, Holland D. "Reading for Social Meaning." *English Journal* 25.3 (1936): 200–05. Print.

Romano, Susan. "The Egalitarianism Narrative: Whose Story? Which Yardstick?" *Computers and Composition* 10.3 (1993): 5–28. Print.

Rossier, Charles W. "The Shift of Values in the Teaching of English." *English Journal* 22.1 (1933): 25–31. Print.

Rouzie, Albert. *At Play in the Fields of Writing: A Serio-Ludic Rhetoric.* Cresskill: Hampton, 2005. Print.

Royster, Jacqueline Jones. "When the First Voice You Hear Is Not Your Own." *College Composition and Communication* 47.1 (1996): 29–40. Print.

Russell, David R. "Vygotsky, Dewey, and Externalism: Beyond the Student/Discipline Dichotomy." *Journal of Advanced Composition* 13.1 (1993): 173–97. Print.

Sackett, S. J. "Report on a Trial of the Oregon Plan." *College English* 22.1 (1960): 45–46. Print.

Sánchez-Casal, Susan, and Amie A. Macdonald. "Introduction: Feminist Reflections on the Pedagogical Relevance of Identity." Macdonald and Sánchez-Casal 1–30.

Sasaki, Betty. "Toward a Pedagogy of Coalition." Macdonald and Sánchez-Casal 31–58.

Scering, Grace E. Sikes. "Themes of a Critical/Feminist Pedagogy: Teacher Education for Democracy." *Journal of Teacher Education* 48.1 (1997): 62–68. Print.

Schneider, Stephen. "Freedom Schooling: Stokely Carmichael and Critical Rhetorical Education." *College Composition and Communication* 58.1 (2006): 46–69. Print.

Schniedewind, Nancy. "Teaching Feminist Process." *Women's Studies Quarterly* 15.3–4 (1987): 15–31. Print.

———. "Teaching Feminist Process in the 1990s." *Women's Studies Quarterly* 21.3–4 (1993): 17–30. Print.

Scholes, Robert. *Textual Power: Literary Theory and the Teaching of English.* New Haven: Yale UP, 1985. Print.

Schultz, John. "The Story Workshop Method: Writing from Start to Finish." *College English* 39.4 (1977): 411–36. Print.

Scott, Linda. Personal conversation.

Shaughnessy, Mina P. *Errors and Expectations: A Guide for the Teacher of Basic Writing.* New York: Oxford UP, 1977. Print.

Sherwood, John C. "The Oregon Experiment: A Final Report." *College Composition and Communication* 9.1 (1958): 5–9. Print.

Shiflett, Betty. "Story Workshop as a Method of Teaching Writing." *College English* 35.2 (1973): 141–60. Print.

Shih, Shu-mei, Sylvia Marcos, Obioma Nnaemeka, and Marguerite Waller. "Conversation on 'Feminist Imperialism and the Politics of Difference.'" Waller and Marcos 143–62.

Shohat, Ella. Introduction. *Talking Visions: Multicultural Feminism in a Transnational Age.* Ed. Shohat. New York: MIT P, 2001. 1–62. Print.

Shor, Ira. *Culture Wars: School and Society in the Conservative Restoration, 1969–1984.* Boston: Routledge, 1986. Print.

———. "Learning How to Learn: Conceptual Teaching in a Course called 'Utopia.'" *College English* 38.7 (1977): 640–47. Print.

———. *When Students Have Power: Negotiating Authority in a Critical Pedagogy.* Chicago: U of Chicago P, 1996. Print.

Shrewsbury, Carolyn M. "What Is Feminist Pedagogy?" *Women's Stud-*

ies Quarterly 15.3–4 (1987): 6–14. Rpt. in *Women's Studies Quarterly* 21.3–4 (1993): 8–16. Print.

Sirc, Geoffrey Michael. *English Composition as a Happening.* Logan: Utah State UP, 2002. Print.

———. "English Composition as a Happening II, Part One." *Pre/Text* 15.3-4 (1994): 264–93. Print.

Sirc, Jeffrey [Geoffrey], and Tom Reynolds. "The Face of Collaboration in the Networked Writing Classroom." Spec. issue of *Computers and Composition Online* 7 (1990): 53–70. Web. 2 May 2017.

Sledd, James. "A Comment on 'Social Construction, Language, and the Authority of Knowledge' and 'A Polemical History of Freshman Composition in Our Time.'" *College English* 49.5 (1987): 585–88. Print.

Smith, Dora V. "American Youth and English." *English Journal* 26.2 (1937): 99–113. Print.

Smitherman, Geneva. "CCCC's Role in the Struggle for Language Rights." *College Composition and Communication* 50.3 (1999): 349–76. Print.

Snipes, Wilson Currin. "An Inquiry: Peer Group Teaching in Freshman Writing." *College Composition and Communication* 22.2 (1971): 169–74. Print.

Sorensen, Frederick. "New Methods in Freshman English." *College English* 14.3 (1952): 161–63. Print.

Spear, Karen. *Sharing Writing: Peer Response Groups in English Classes.* Portsmouth: Heinemann, 1988. Print.

Springsteen, Bruce. "We Are Alive." *Wrecking Ball.* Columbia, 2012. CD.

Squire, James R. "English at the Crossroads: The 'National Interest' Report plus Eighteen." *English Journal* 51.6 (1962): 381–92. Print.

Sterling, Richard. "Bruffee and the CUNY Circle." *Writing Center Journal* 28.2 (2008): 19–24. Print.

Stewart, Donald C. "Collaborative Learning and Composition: Boon or Bane?" *Rhetoric Review* 7.1 (1988): 58–83. Print.

Stolper, B. J. R. "The Group Poem: An Experiment in a New Sort of Verse." *English Journal* 27.4 (1938): 311–22. Print.

Students' Right to Their Own Language. Spec. issue of *College Composition and Communication* 25.3 (1974): 1–32. Print.

Sutherland, Robert D. "Letting Students Be: Report on a Continuing Experiment in Education." *College English* 32.7 (1971): 733–39. Print.

Tekobbe, Cindy, Yazmin Lazcano-Pry, and Duane Roen. "Collaborative Learning and Writing in Digital Environments." *Collaborative Learning and Writing: Essays on Using Small Groups in Teaching English and Composition.* Ed. Kathleen M. Hunzer. Jefferson: McFarland, 2012. 87–98. Print.

Trimbur, John. "Collaborative Learning and Teaching Writing." *Perspectives on Research and Scholarship in Composition.* Ed. Ben W. McClelland and Timothy R. Donovan. New York: MLA, 1985. 87–109. Print.

———. "Composition and the Circulation of Writing." *College Composition and Communication* 52.2 (2000): 188–219. Print.

———. "Consensus and Difference in Collaborative Learning." *College English* 51.6 (1989): 602–16. Print.

———. "Multiliteracies, Social Futures, and Writing Centers." *Writing Center Journal* 30.1 (2010): 88–91. Print.

———. "Paper Trails: The Brooklyn College Institute for Training Peer Writing Tutors and the Composition Archive." *Writing Center Journal* 28.2 (2008): 72–79. Print.

———. "The Politics of Radical Pedagogy: A Plea for 'A Dose of Vulgar Marxism.'" Rev. of *Border Crossings: Cultural Workers and the Politics of Education,* by Henry A. Giroux, *Beyond the Culture Wars: How Teaching the Conflicts Can Revitalize American Education,* by Gerald Graff, *Composition and Resistance,* ed. C. Mark Hurlbert and Michael Blitz, *Empowering Education: Critical Teaching for Social Change,* by Ira Shor, and *Education Limited: School and Training and the New Right since 1979,* by Education Group II, Cultural Studies, U of Birmingham. *College English* 56.2 (1994): 194–206. Print.

Trinh T. Minh-ha. "Not You/Like You: Postcolonial Women and the Interlocking Questions of Identity and Difference." 1988. *The Longman Anthology of Women's Literature.* Ed. Mary K. DeShazer. New York: Longman, 2001. 928–33. Print.

United States. Dept. of Health, Education, and Welfare. Office of Education. "Project English." *College Composition and Communication* 13.1 (1962): 39–42. Print.

"Using Group Dynamics in Teaching Composition/Communication." *College Composition and Communication* 8.3 (1957): 150–51. Print.

Vetter, Matthew. "Composing with *Wikipedia*: A Classroom Study of Online Writing." *Computers and Composition Online* (Virtual Classroom Section, Winter 2013): n. pag. Web. 2 May 2017.

———. "Teaching Wikipedia: The Pedagogy and Politics of an Open Access Writing Community." Diss. Ohio University, 2015. Print.

Villanueva, Victor. "The Rhetorics of Racism: A Historical Sketch." *Writing Centers and the New Racism: A Call for Sustainable Dialogue and Change.* Ed. Laura Greenfield and Karen Rowan. Logan: Utah State UP, 2011. 17–32. Print.

Waks, Leonard J. "John Dewey and the Challenge of Progressive Education." *International Journal of Progressive Education* 9.1 (2013): 73–83. Web. 8 May 2017.

Waller, Marguerite. "'One Voice Kills Both Our Voices': 'First World' Feminism and Transcultural Feminist Engagement." Waller and Marcos 113–42.

———. Waller, Marguerite, and Sylvia Marcos, eds. *Dialogue and Difference: Feminisms Challenge Globalization.* New York: Palgrave, 2005. Print.

Ward, Frank Earl. "Modern World Culture: An Experiment in Correlation with History." *English Journal* College Ed. 20.7 (1931): 580–88. Print.

———. "Social Ideals in Freshman English." *English Journal* 19.4 (1930): 297–307. Print.

Webb, Lynne M., Myria W. Allen, and Kandi L. Walker. "Feminist Pedagogy: Identifying Basic Principles." *Academic Exchange Quarterly* 6.1 (2002): 67–72. Print.

Wendt, Allan. "Who's a Yahoo!" *College English* 33.3 (1971): 317–23. Print.

Westbrook, Robert B. *John Dewey and American Democracy.* Ithaca: Cornell UP, 1991. Print.

Wiener, Harvey S. "Collaborative Learning in the Classroom: A Guide to Evaluation." *College English* 48.1 (1986): 52–61. Print.

"Wikipedia: Five Pillars." *Wikipedia: The Free Encyclopedia.* Wikimedia Foundation. 13 July 2015. Web. 20 July 2015.

Wikipedia: The Free Encyclopedia. Wikimedia Foundation. 14 Aug. 2017. Web. 23 Aug. 2013.

Winkelmann, Carol L. "Electronic Literacy, Critical Pedagogy, and Collaboration: A Case for Cyborg Writing." *Computers and the Humanities* 29.6 (1995): 431–48. Print.

Winter, Sara. "The Unalienated Teacher." *College English* 33.3 (1971): 268–76. Print.

Wolf, H. R. "The Classroom as Microcosm." *College English* 33.3 (1971): 259–67. Print.

———. "Composition and Group Dynamics: The Paradox of Freedom." *College English* 30.6 (1969): 441–44. Print.

Wykoff, George S. "Current Solutions for Teaching Maximum Numbers with Limited Faculty." *College Composition and Communication* 9.2 (1958): 76–80. Print.

Wysocki, Anne Frances, Johndan Johnson-Eilola, Cynthia L. Selfe, and Geoffrey Sirc. *Writing New Media: Theory and Applications for Expanding the Teaching of Composition*. Logan: Utah State UP, 2004. *JStor*. Web. 1 May 2017.

Youdelman, Jeffrey. "Limiting Students: Remedial Writing and the Death of Open Admissions." *College English* 39.5 (1978): 562–72. Print.

Zappen, James P., Laura J. Gurak, and Stephen Doheny-Farina. "Rhetoric, Community, and Cyberspace." *Rhetoric Review* 15.2 (1997): 400–19. Print.

Zuckerman, Galina A. "A Pilot Study of a Ten-Day Course in Cooperative Learning for Beginning Russian First Graders." *Elementary School Journal* 94.4 (1994): 405–20. Print.

INDEX

AUTHOR

Mara Holt is associate professor of English at Ohio University, where she teaches graduate and undergraduate students, directs dissertations, and serves as director of composition. Some of the journals she has published in are *College Composition and Communication*, *JAC*, *Pre/text*, and *Profession*. Her current project involves incorporating racial literacies into the first-year English curriculum. In 1980 and 1983 she was a fellow of the Brooklyn College Institute in Peer Tutor Training and Collaborative Learning, sponsored by the Fund for the Improvement of Postsecondary Education, directed by Kenneth Bruffee and evaluated by Peter Elbow. She subsequently developed peer-tutor training programs at Alabama State University and Embry-Riddle Aeronautical University before moving to Texas and earning her PhD at the University of Texas at Austin.

BOOKS IN THE CCCC STUDIES IN WRITING & RHETORIC SERIES

This book was typeset in Garamond and Frutiger by Barbara Frazier.
Typefaces used on the cover include Adobe Garamond and Calibri.
The book was printed on 55-lb. Natural Offset paper
by King Printing Company, Inc.

www.ingramcontent.com/pod-product-compliance
Lightning Source LLC
Chambersburg PA
CBHW050714280326
41926CB00088B/3026